WHEN OUR CHILDREN
COME OUT

AGENCE LITTERAIRE
LORA FOUNTAIN & ASSOCIATES
7, rue de Belfort-75011 Paris
Tél : (33) 01 43 56 21 96

Dedication

This book is dedicated to all parents and families
who support and cherish their GLBT children.

In particular, this book is for Nan McGregor and Mollie Smith
and the many other parents and families of
Australian PFLAGs.

WHEN OUR CHILDREN

COME OUT

How to support gay, lesbian, bisexual and transgendered young people

Maria Pallotta-Chiarolli

FINCH PUBLISHING
SYDNEY

When Our Children Come Out

This edition first published in 2005 in Australia and New Zealand by Finch Publishing Pty Limited, PO Box 120, Lane Cove, NSW 1595, Australia. ABN 49 057 285 248

07 06 05   8 7 6 5 4 3 2 1

National Library of Australia Cataloguing-in-Publication entry
Pallotta-Chiarolli, Maria.
When our children come out: how to support gay, lesbian,
bisexual and transgendered young people.

Includes index.
ISBN 1 876451 44 0.

1. Coming out (Sexual orientation). 2. Gays - Family relationships. 3. Bisexuals - Family relationships. 4. Transsexuals - Family relationships. 5. Heterosexual parents - Attitudes. I. Title.

306.76

Edited by Heather Jamieson
Editorial assistance from Rosemary Peers
Text designed and typeset in Melior and Officiana Sans by saso content and design
Cover design by saso content and design
Cover photographs courtesy of Margaret Ainsworth, Jamie Dunbar, Pam Garske,
    Nan McGregor and Karla Mokros.
Illustrations by Kenton Miller, except p. 131 by Bonnie, p. 133 by Jackie Ruddock,
    and p. 199 by John of YGLAM.
Printed by Southwood Press

Notes The 'Author's notes' section at the back of this book contains useful additional information and references to quoted material in the text. Each reference is linked to the text by its relevant page number and an identifying line entry.

Photo credits Jamie Dunbar, Dianne Jeffrey, Sam Trigg and contributors.

Note concerning the contributors Every reasonable effort has been made by the editor to ensure that the edited versions of written contributions were submitted to the writers for their approval. Many of the contributors have used pseudonyms and have altered other identifying details in order to protect their own and other people's confidentiality and anonymity.

Other Finch titles can be viewed at www.finch.com.au

Contents

Foreword

'Coming out' is a life-long process. Heterosexual people do not 'come out' as such. But those, like me, in the GLBT minority of the population make that journey. They do so in their homes, with their families, in their schools, at work or before the whole world. Some do so only in their own minds and think they keep their 'secret' entirely to themselves because there are others who hate to hear the truth. But it is the truth that makes us free. This is a book to help those with same-gender sexual attractions, their families, teachers and friends to understand the 'coming out' process so that its traumas are reduced, so far as that is humanly possible. No one should make the journey completely alone.

The good feature of this book is that so much of it is expressed in the words of people who have made the journey of coming out: gays, lesbians, bisexuals, transsexuals and other members of sexual minorities and their families, friends and teachers. Theory is all very well. Research is important. It was, after all, the research of Dr Alfred Kinsey and his successors that showed the wide variety of the human sexual response and the proportion of the population that does not fit easily, or at all, into the binary division earlier assumed to be universal.

But in the end, in securing understanding and a rational human reaction, it is essential to tell human stories. Everyone who has walked this way has their own story. It may be locked away in their mind or it may be out and about for all to see. The pain and cruelty of denying the imprint of one's nature is so horrible that it is scarcely imaginable that today there are still people who want to force others back into the binary taxonomy that is unnatural for them. Yet such people exist. They exist in religious bodies, in politics, out there in the suburbs, even in the law that promises equal justice for all. However, things are getting better, at least in educated and informed societies like Australia. Knowledge, rationality and human stories are the change-agents. The rediscovery of the essentially spiritual lesson of love, which lies behind the fundamentals of all religions, promises a better future.

Meantime, there is work to be done in helping young people to cope with discoveries about themselves that are deep and serious and very personal. At the time of such discoveries, you can take it from me, young people need help, love and support. This book, through the words of parents, teachers, grandparents and friends, as well as of those most affected, will assist those for whom this journey is a puzzle to understand it better and to accomplish it with the dignity, intelligence and grace that represent the best of our human nature.

In my day, at school, absolutely nothing was said about sexuality. Total and complete silence. Nothing much was said at home. They were the ways of those times. Even in the playground, apart from occasional jibes at 'poofters', nothing much was said. Don't ask, don't tell was the rule. For most of my life, I complied.

In due course, my father, my brothers and sister and I broached the subject. As expected, their response was one of loving acceptance. All of them had truly understood the central message of the religion in which we were raised. As one of the contributors to this book points out, God or nature does not make mistakes in things so basic. With my mother, I never directly discussed the matter until shortly before her death six years ago. By then, it was a rather antique 'confession'. When I spoke the words, she looked at me with her beautiful, intelligent eyes and said: 'Michael, what do you take me for? You've been bringing Johan to dinner for 30 years. Get real.' So I have and I will.

The stories in this book will raise a tear. For many readers, dark fears and cruel times will come flooding back. Some stories will make the reader angry and upset. Some will cause a sense of admiration. All will help us to understand the journey that begins with the perceptions of an individual, spreads through the family, the school, the workplace and wider still until truth and rationality encompass the whole world.

The full journey of coming out will not be completed in our lifetimes. But it has begun. It will not be reversed. Science teaches that a small proportion of every population is outside the binary division of sexual orientation. Increasingly, we know judges and artists, footballers and rock stars, garbage collectors and air pilots, politicians and sweepers whose sexual orientation is different from the majority. They are not going away. Most, if not all, cannot change. They have families, mortgages, pets and, if they are lucky like me, life companions. They are citizens, taxpayers, individual human beings and part of God's or nature's creation.

All of us have to understand these truths and adjust to this reality. And you should never forget that the law is there to protect everyone. This book is a gentle companion to help us, whatever our sexuality, to 'get real'.

The Hon Justice Michael Kirby AC CMG
Canberra
1 October 2004

Who can I tell?

Pamela Du Valle

Who can I tell that my child is Gay?
Oh my God what will they say?
Telling my friends about my son,
I knew I just could not tell anyone.

I had to pick the time and the place,
And openly tell them face to face.
My heart would be scared and skip a beat inside,
As I tried to explain, yet wanting to hide.

Who can I tell, who will accept me as I am?
Boy it must be hell on my young man.
To keep a secret deep in one's soul,
For society says being Gay is not whole.

Who can I tell? Who can I tell?
For young Gay people it must be hell
As who can I tell is my story too,
Who can I tell? Will it be you?

Will you still accept myself and my son?
Or do you just want to leave and run?
Run from the truth of another human being,
Like it is never to be heard or never be seen.

Well, I will tell you now and it is up to you,
To my son and myself I have to be true.
If you do not accept myself and my son,
Our friendship is over, over and done.

So believe it or not, it is up to you,
My son comes first and to him I am true.
True to him as any Mother can be,
My son is GAY, HAPPY, REAL and FREE.

My son came out of the closet and I went right in

Pamela Du Valle

My son was hiding a secret from about the age of nine. He was attracted to other boys but didn't know how to tell me.

It crossed my mind many times that my son could be gay. I actually collected articles about it and hid them in my cupboard. Why I did that, I'm still not sure, as I hadn't had anything to do with homosexuality and didn't know anyone who was gay.

When he was nineteen, my son told me over the phone he was gay. I was very cool to him and said, 'That's okay'.

But I got off the phone and burst into tears.

It was like my son came out of the closet and I went right in – and closed the door for two weeks. I was alone and I didn't know who to talk to. So I wrote the poem you've just read: 'Who Can I Tell?' That made me feel better. I then phoned around all the community places I could find and eventually found a mothers' group. This helped me greatly as it was nice to know I wasn't the only one. All the fears of my child's health and safety came into action. I'd lie awake worrying about AIDS, my son getting bashed, or just abused by society in general. It was a very tough time.

I began to attend various workshops and even went dancing and clubbing with my son and his friends. This opened a very special place in my heart, and it was an opportunity to get to really know the gay community and all the hopes, dreams and fears they carry through life. My relationship with my son became closer, and his friends became my friends. I'm often seen as a mother figure to those caring, thoughtful and sensitive young men who do not have supportive parents and family.

So if you find out your child is gay, love them, ask them questions, and admire them for the courage to tell you.

Take care, all the best.

Introduction:

When our children come out

You can't love them today
then find out they're gay
and then you don't love them any more tomorrow.

A mum

Welcome to a world where adults support and affirm their gay, lesbian, bisexual and transgendered young people!

In this book, you're going to be hearing from parents, families, teachers, religious and ethnic community members and young people themselves. They share their stories and strategies, the pleasures and pain, the laughter and tears, that go with you when young people come out as non-heterosexual, gay, lesbian, bisexual or transgendered (from now on referred to as GLBT for the sake of convenience and inclusivity!).

In putting together this book, I had one question: *How are you supporting GLBT young people in your family, your school and your communities?*

Extraordinary ordinary people responded, spoke out, opened their lives and their hearts for you in this book so that you can feel strengthened in supporting the coming out of your children.

The contributors to this book tell us that supporting GLBT young people means:

▶▶ families being a loving haven for raising healthy and happy GLBT children

▶▶ schools including sexual diversity and gender diversity in their promotion and celebration of social justice and equity, multiculturalism and social diversity

▶▶ religious groups calling for GLBT young people to be explicitly included in the basic values of love, respect, and the dignity of each individual.

Contributors also tell us that supporting our children when they come out means **refusing**:

Refusing to do nothing

▶▶ Not ignoring that moment in the family lounge room when a homophobic ad comes on the TV and everyone just laughs along at the 'faggots'.

▶▶ Not side-stepping the incident in the school hallway where some students are yelling out 'Sue is a lezo' at a young woman caught with a photo of her girlfriend.

▶▶ Not squashing GLBT young people from the pulpit by telling them they'll burn in hell.

▶▶ Not excusing the local lads in your small town who have almost drowned 'the town tranny' in a rainwater tank by saying 'that's just boys being boys'.

Refusing to accept it's the child's problem

Just like the 'problem' of racism is not being a particular ethnicity or skin colour, but the ways that others react to it, the 'problem' of homophobia is not being GLBT.

The 'problem' is *heteronormativity*: the political, institutional and social acceptance that discrimination, exploitation and exclusion of GLBT people is 'normal' and justified. Unfortunately, though, the problem of heteronormativity does become a problem for GLBT young people. They have to deal with the manifestations of heteronormativity, commonly known as homophobia and heterosexism.

Refusing to accept that having a GLBT child is something to 'cope with', 'grieve over', 'come to terms with'

I'm saddened by this kind of language – as if the child has a deficit or an abnormality that we have to 'get used to' and 'help' the young person 'live with'! Sure, many parents in this book do speak about experiencing these reactions. But they also talk about moving on from this initial point to asking:

'*Why* does society, religion, politics and culture try to convince me that my child has a deficit or an abnormality?'

'*How* can my child live happily and healthily in a world with such prejudice and ignorance?'

'*What* can I do to keep making the world a better place for my child and all GLBT children?'

Thus, the parents and others in this book talk about going beyond 'tolerance' and 'acceptance' to affirmation and celebration.

Refusing to deny your responsibility as adults for the health and wellbeing of GLBT young people

Just as it's our adult, heteronormative world that makes GLBT young people's daily lives too often filled with darkness, it's our responsibility to get them back into the sunshine.

Times are changing: there's a new generation of GLBT young people coming out at a younger age, and a new generation of parents whose children are more likely to come out to them rather than hide it from them. These generations of both kids and their parents (as well as teachers and communities) have more information and exposure to sexual diversity through the media and popular culture – even though not all of it is positive or useful! Fewer parents want to 'fix the problem' and more want to 'work together' to support their child and the family. These parents don't want society to rob them of their child. They know that parents who cut off their relationship with their child pay a heavy price: they can push their son and/or daughter out of their lives, but not out of their hearts.

The parents and others in this book are realistic, though. They know that supporting and affirming GLBT young people may mean taking the personal, social, and professional risks involved in challenging homophobia. They're not dismissing or trivialising how difficult it can be. But, in conducting interviews, facilitating discussion groups, and calling for contributions for this book, I've been inspired and humbled by the many dynamic parents, teachers, ethnic community members, youth workers, religious leaders and young people themselves who have decided it's time to take that risk, and the more people who do, the less risky it becomes!

By the end of this book, I trust and hope you'll be:

▶▶ provided with basketfuls of ideas and strategies

▶▶ encouraged with questions, and encouraged to ask questions

▶▶ moved to tears and to laughter, inspired and affirmed to support GLBT young people in your own families, schools and communities.

Most of all, you'll know that you're not alone. More and more people are coming out against a homophobic society. They're stepping forward cautiously, making leaps bravely, and turning corners quietly.

I hope this book and its messages of hope, strength and action go with you on your journey.

I wouldn't change my son for anything
Pamela Garske

I'm the mother of two children, a homosexual son and a heterosexual daughter. I wonder why I make that distinction. My gay son is good-looking, has lots of friends, is single, has a job, pays rent, wishes for a mortgage. My straight daughter is also attractive, has lots of friends and is engaged to a very special person, has a job, pays board, wishes for a mortgage. One day I will hopefully have two sons-in-law. What either of my children do in their bedroom is none of my business but both of them and their friends are always welcome in our home.

What's the difference between my children that makes them get treated differently? The gender of the person they're attracted to.

In the early years, our son was very easy-going, very friendly, played easily with other children and loved school. He was very bright, attended Cubs, then Scouts and a drama group. Adults generally thought he was delightful. Our daughter was a more challenging child to raise. She was friendly, attended Brownies and learnt music, finally joining a youth band.

As our son got older, he only had a couple of close male friends as his peers generally found him 'different'. But he had loads of gorgeous girlfriends. My son was elected school captain in Year 6. The teachers were thrilled, as were my husband and myself. Some kids at school booed him. Why, we wondered.

Boys started calling him 'Gaylord', which hurt. I tried to explain to him and to myself that they didn't know what they were saying, but they certainly knew it was derogatory, and that it hurt. Was I to blame for all this because I was an older mother (for those days)? Was I dressing him 'differently'? Was it the little rag doll he had as a baby? So many questions and concerns, but I kept them to myself.

High school was a nightmare for our son. On one occasion he went missing, the school phoned, and I spent the latter half of the day walking his route to school looking in bushes and calling his name, wondering what he was hiding from. He eventually arrived home. He'd spent the day with a sympathetic friend. He said he just couldn't face another day of harassment at school. His self-esteem was almost non-existent and he never smiled.

Why did my son's peers harass him? What was 'different' about him? I knew something was 'different' when comparing him to other boys. What should I do about it? Why wasn't my daughter treated the same way by her peers? 'I must've been too protective towards my son,' I tried to rationalise.

After he was hit in the head with a chair, we moved him to another school. I soon came to realise the 'problem' was my son himself. It was at this time I wondered if he was gay. 'What will I do if he is?' I thought to myself.

Our home life was suffering as well. He was moody, withdrawn, dark, and his paintings and drawings depicted death. I felt sure he would commit suicide. So I took him to an adolescent psychologist who suggested he might be gay but was still sorting himself out. I felt I'd rather have a gay son than a dead son, so I was a little relieved.

At the age of fifteen, he left high school and did a Fine Arts course. The harassment didn't stop. He was attacked on public transport, and while sitting at the bus stop; and we had graffiti on our property.

Finally he left home with our blessing and with the help of boxes of food. He had had enough.

Our son eventually came out. It wasn't news to me. It was to my husband, who was wonderful. The coming out experience for us was quite public as we agreed to be part of an article in the newspaper. We gave it so much thought but as it was something our son wanted to do we decided he meant more to us than neighbours, friends or even relatives. What a liberating experience it turned out to be. The fear of what people would say disappeared very quickly. The most interesting thing that did happen was people stopped asking questions. All along they knew something was 'different'. Now they knew the answer and stopped asking, 'Has he got a girlfriend?', 'When is he getting married?' or 'Where is he?'

I wouldn't change my son for anything. A person's sexuality is one of the many colours that make up the rainbow of humanity. Homosexuality is not an illness. I think the world would be so much the poorer if there were no gays.

I believe education is the most important issue. I'm part of panels that go to schools to talk about sexuality and homophobia. Sometimes I'm concerned at the homophobia which still exists today. One student asked me if I had felt my son was 'different', why didn't I do something to change him. I asked, 'Where should I have gone?', to which she replied,

'There must be somewhere. As his mother, you should know.' At another school, one student passed the comment that if her parents knew what was on at school that day she wouldn't have been allowed to attend.

My husband also spreads the anti-homophobia message. He works in a blue-collar job and homophobia is rife, but as opportunities arise he never lets them go. One day at a work Christmas party, a young gay man greeted his partner with a kiss on the cheek, to which a couple of others made some typical homophobic remarks. My husband went up to one of them and kissed him on top of his bald head. He then asked, 'Did that hurt?'

I never let any homophobic comment pass. During lunch, one of the casual workers at my job didn't know about my son and she was becoming quite homophobic. I informed her about my son and how proud I was of him, to which she replied, 'I feel so sorry for you.' A couple of weeks later, she indicated she wished to speak to me and said, 'I want to thank you for opening my eyes on homosexuality.' She'd gone home and started reading and realised how little she really knew. I was thrilled. I believe if I can make just one person stop and think about their attitude then I've achieved something.

My plan for the future is to keep talking to whoever will listen, to participate in as many educational panels as I'm able, and to do my very best to see a less homophobic society.

The Garske family

Part 1:

When our children come out in families

For many GLBT young people, the time they're thinking about their sexuality and gender also becomes the time when the home they've known as a place of love, safety and nurturing threatens to become a place of abuse, fear and shame. Lauren's poem, below, so powerfully tells us how devastating and detrimental it is to a young person's health and wellbeing to find that they have become a stranger in what they had always seen as their sanctuary! Is this the kind of experience of 'home' that we want our GLBT young people to take into their adult lives?

In this section, we will hear from many parents and families who have made sure that their GLBT young people will always have a 'home' within which to feel supported, safe and strengthened against the outside world.

Home is not my own
Lauren

There was a time in which
this place meant the world to me
It was my sanctuary
my place for me to be
But now time has opened my eyes
This place is deaf to all my cries
I don't know where I am
but I know it's not my home
When I was young and lonely
this place would give me life
But now that I'm grown and wise
it cuts me like a knife
I now see that the end is near
I simply can no longer stay here
I don't know where I am
but I know it's not my home
So as I cry these tears
and wish to be afar
It's not to be mean, dear father
but I'll follow my own star
This place it gave me all it can give
but I must leave so I can continue to live
Because I don't know where I am
but I know it's not my home ...

> *My father – I don't call him Dad because he isn't one – always told me I was nothing. I think he thought that me being gay just proved that. One day he'll realise that he's missing out on his son growing into a man, but it may be too late by then.* **Dave**

> *One day they'll wake up and realise that they're in danger of losing their only daughter. Maybe then they'll be ready to talk.* **Jaimie**

If it isn't easy to talk the words, write them!

Adele and Ted Shaheed

Hi, I'm Adele, and I'm the mother of a gay son. I'm also a teacher, and the student welfare coordinator at my school. Here are three letters that transpired within the first 72 hours after Ted's coming out last year when he was sixteen. His partner John, nineteen, was present when Ted came out to me. John was also my older daughter's best friend.

One of the letters you're going to read is from myself to my son 48 hours after he came out. It's partly an apology, partly a confession of my unconditional love. I'm not altogether proud of some of the reactions I talk about in my letter, but I offer it to you as an example of the mistakes, processes, pain and joy in one family's coming out experience.

Dear Mum,

I'm writing to you because when we talk we don't seem to get very far.

I realise that I have expected too much from you to deal with this easily. Of course you have concerns and I expect you to. Please understand, with time we will both be better off. We will have an honest relationship and I will not be lying to you every day.

I should have considered where you're at in your life and maybe postponed the news. But at the same time, it felt right to tell you when I did. I am not asking you to be happy or understand me for a while, but please try to accept my decision, as I know you are.

It is/will be hard for you to lie to those you are most fond of and that's one of my major regrets. But it was hard for me to lie to the person I've loved most for such a long time –

you. I am not changing, nor must our relationship. It will be tough through these initial months – but things can only improve. And no matter what I/we go through, you will always be the figure in my life who I look up to – who I respect the most.

There is no-one to blame here – and be angry with me if you must, but not John. John has helped me, not forced me. And I ask that you keep your original thoughts about John as they were. He is not to blame. But neither are you. You blaming yourself is very upsetting for me as I know I have always been like this, and it's not through role-modelling, etc.

I do not regret telling you. If you saw me in bed some nights before I told you, you'd be glad too. Some nights I would cry myself to sleep, sick of living a lie. Sick of doing things I hated doing because I wanted to fit in. Now I am only crying for you.

I respect any decisions you will make, although not agreeing with them.
It's killing me to see you like this, but I understand.
I love you so much, and that will definitely never change.
Love, your son,

Ted.

Dear Ted,

It's important for me to write some stuff down. Hope you don't mind.

From the small amount of reading I've done, it's clear that my initial reactions in these first days is very common. Being common, however, does not excuse outbursts. I am deeply sorry.

I was, and am, in shock. From counselling studies and life experiences, I know there will be other stages which I will no doubt weave my way through.

I realise that much soul-searching and probably years of turmoil led to last Monday evening. Telling me will be one of the greatest hurdles you shall face in life. It took immense strength and courage. I am overwhelmed with admiration and affection.

I am proud of you for being the person you are – in every way. I could not ask for better children.

Never ever will I be ashamed or embarrassed. When the time comes, if or when you are ready, I will have no difficulty, none whatsoever, in laying the cards on the table. I will stand tall and proud.

For the immediate future (and these are my own personal uninfluenced feelings):

- *I believe it's important to eliminate the words 'fault' and 'blame' from our vocabulary. Nobody here is at fault or guilty.*
- *I would like you to stop apologising, for you have done nothing wrong. You have not hurt me. On the contrary, I am honoured you were willing to approach me.*
- *I would also like to go over how I felt that you didn't consider timing (my work deadlines, operation, etc). Well, that is bullshit – I'm the parent here. When the time is right for you, I should be there. I'm sorry for being so self-centred.*

The timing was perfect (and hey, I managed work).
If ever you need me, don't ever consider my agenda.
Never. *I am always available for you and your sister*
Corina. I'm human, I do react, but I eventually discover
means of coping.

- In my own defence, it was too much too soon and I cannot
yet get my head around a relationship. However, I intend to
do some mending where John is concerned.

There is much relief – that you spoke to Corina and me
when you did – when you felt ready. Relief that hopefully
you will start to feel happier about yourself and more confi-
dent among your peers. Hopefully, much confusion and
anxiety will be greatly diminished for you. I would like you
to talk to me about what it's been like for you over however
many years. I need to know.

My plans:

- To continue to maintain and enjoy our happy home life.
I cannot foresee changes – work, school, chores, leisure –
your honesty could in fact enhance an existing solid base.
There will be turbulent times just like in all families for all
sorts of reasons, but we will manage.
- To educate myself by reading, questioning, talking. I will
attend PFLAG meetings and read through all the literature
I've asked them to send. You will have to understand that
it's vital that parents associate with other parents in similar
circumstances. Information is empowering for you, for me,
for all parties.
- Eventually, I will be pleased to meet and open our home to
any new friends you will meet.
    It sounds so clichéd, but I do love you and Corina uncon-
ditionally. This does not mean I won't experience anger or

disappointment, just as you do with me, for any variety of reasons. We have so much to celebrate and be thankful for. If it is remotely possible, this past week has heightened my love even more – you for your strength, courage, honesty, and concern for me; and Corina for her logic, calmness, and undying loyalty to both of us.

Finally, I firmly believe that this revelation is the first major step to what will become for you a happier, successful and fulfilling life. It could not be delayed any longer. Instinct, gut feeling – follow it and you can't go far wrong.
Thank you for being such an exceptional son.
I love you always,

Mum.

Dear John,

I believe you've heard that I've been experiencing much anxiety, and I also believe you deserve an explanation.
Last Monday night, I was in deep shock, and likely overreacted. Although still very much in a headspin, I am somewhat calmer now. Nevertheless, you should probably know what my thoughts were during these last days.
In hindsight, I became very angry that Ted had stayed out all night the previous Friday, and that ultimately led to his being 'pushed'. A few days down the track, I realise that his being and talking with you was a good thing. It was so important that he tell me. However, it's unacceptable that a sixteen-year-old stay out all night without asking or letting us know his whereabouts. But that is Ted's mistake – and we all make mistakes.

Then it hit me like a bullet on Tuesday that you had your own agenda on Monday – an ulterior motive: that you wanted to be involved with Ted, therefore couldn't wait to tell me. Again, I overreacted. I would like to believe that you were simply being supportive at a profoundly difficult time.

Nevertheless, to discover my son is gay and to consider there might already be a love interest, my daughter's friend, was too much information too soon. Having since spoken to a few counsellors and having done some reading, again it's clear that my reactions have been typical.

So where do we stand? I would hope:

- *For Corina and Ted to be happy and comfortable. For all of their friends to feel welcome to phone or come over.*
- *For you to remain a close friend to them, but at the same time, understand that I need time to get my head around countless concerns.*
- *That you continue to support both Corina and Ted in the best way you know how, provided that it's not too much of an imposition, too big an ask.*

You do not need to be scared of seeing me or hesitant to phone or come around. You were told and now you have read about my confusion – best it's all out. But bottom line – I do see that you were being supportive and if Ted was, in fact, influenced to tell Corina and myself, that's a positive outcome.

Take care, John. We'll see you soon,

Adele.

I feel blessed that I have a gay child

Pam Cooke

I feel blessed that I have had a gay child as it's opened my eyes.
My world has expanded and my love for Joanne, my daughter, has
grown far more than I ever realised it would. To get to this point,
the road hasn't been easy, but the journey certainly has been very
worthwhile.

I first wondered about my daughter's sexuality when she was about
thirteen. I discovered, quite by accident, a letter that she'd written to
a girl. I was most upset with its contents. After a lot of soul-searching,
I picked my moment and asked Jo about the letter. She told me that her
and her friend often wrote stupid things in class when they were bored.
I asked her straight out if they were having a lesbian relationship. She
was very adamant that this wasn't the case. Jo then asked me very seriously not to mention this conversation to her father.

After this episode, she had two short interludes with boys and then
there were no 'boyfriends', as such. She was always busy with her
sport and had many good friends associated with this. I tried to put
the subject of her sexuality out of my mind, but it never really left.

It was never discussed again till Jo was eighteen. Once again, I was
tidying her room, emptying the rubbish bin, and noticed a poem that
she'd written. Being a poetry lover, I started to read it and realised that
she'd written this to another girl.

Apart from the fact that I felt I'd invaded Jo's privacy, I was once
again forced to face this issue head on. I knew that I needed to discuss
this with her again and decided to write Jo a letter because I'm a very
emotional person when speaking from the heart and my tears often get
in the way of what I want to say. I had told my husband about the
poem and I spent a couple of days putting the letter together, telling
Jo how much her father and I loved her.

I gave Jo my letter on a night when her brother and father were out.
She read it and came to me crying, saying, 'We need to talk.'

My worst fears were true – she said, 'Yes Mum, I'm gay.'

She told me that she'd known since she was about ten years of age
that she felt different. I was absolutely astounded at this. I was also

very saddened to think of her being so young and not feeling that she was able to come to me and discuss it.

Jo was very defensive when talking to me. This really upset me at the time. But on looking back, I understand that she didn't know what my response would be and she felt that she had to be on guard to protect herself. She said to me, 'Mum, it's really no big deal.' I guess that after knowing for so long and dealing with it herself that it was no big deal for her. But I remember thinking to myself, 'You must be joking, dear – this is a really big deal for me.'

That night was a turning point in my life as a mother, and I'm sure my daughter will never forget that night as long as she lives. Jo's 'coming out' changed all of our lives, but I can honestly say that our lives changed for the better.

For about two years prior to our daughter turning eighteen, she'd become very sullen and withdrawn. Her communication and eye contact with the family was minimal. She was very rude to her father in particular and on many occasions I had to reprimand her. She'd be pleasant for a short time and then revert back to the bad behaviour pattern. After Jo came out to us, we got our old daughter back. With the huge load lifted from her heart, she could now be herself once again. My husband and I rejoiced in the dramatic change that took place.

We made it our business to find out everything we could about homosexuality. I found several books in bookshops and I know I read the first one several times to make it sink in.

We've rid ourselves of all the homophobia that we both were guilty of. We've come to understand that we had both grown up in a society where we learnt a lot of untruths about homosexuality. Coming to understand that my beloved daughter Joanne was gay made me face my own fears and ignorance, and in doing so, changed my whole outlook on life.

I am now a more confident, direct, open person, with greater inner strength. I know this is because I had what I considered at the time to be a crisis in my life, and I faced it head on. It gives me great joy and satisfaction to assist and advise other parents who are where I was in the early days, and to see them move along on their own journey to self-discovery.

So to all you parents, learn all you can about homosexuality. Read as much as you can get your hands on and if you feel the need, seek out a support group. You'll find that to speak to other parents who've shared this experience will be very helpful. As parents of gay children we have to re-educate ourselves. We have to rid ourselves of all the learnt behaviour and bigoted knowledge that we've been taught by society over the years. What a travesty this is on society, that young people who realise that they're homosexual or bisexual are still burdened with so much.

I could go on and on but the most important things are:

▶▶ Focus on the love you have for your child. Remember, they haven't changed – you have.

▶▶ Be gentle on yourself.

▶▶ Learn all you can.

▶▶ Continue to love and support your child as you would've had they been heterosexual.

You will be okay – believe me.
I've been where you are right now.
You'll be fine.
It may just take some time.

Best wishes to you and your family.
Bless our GLBT kids.

We haven't created monsters!

Shirley and Graham Hughes

Shirley: After the initial shock there was a sense of relief. He'd made suicide attempts and we didn't understand why. When Shane said he was bisexual, it clicked. And we thought if we were accepting, maybe it would lessen the threat of suicide.

Graham: I knew he had a lot of trouble at school but I couldn't work it out. I was tied up with work, I just didn't have the time to scratch myself, let alone listen to his problems. So, consequently, I was at fault in that respect in that I put his troubles on the backburner. When I came home from work the day Shane told his mum, Shirley made me a coffee, sat me down, and when she told me, I didn't feel anger. I felt sad. I felt sad that Shane hadn't come to me, too, straight off. But then the greatest feeling was relief to find out what had been bugging him all those years.

Shirley: We had a choice of either accepting or rejecting. By accepting, by looking into it, meeting up with other people, being given the opportunity to do all the great things that we've done, all I can say to other parents is, for God's sake, wake up to yourselves. There is life after gayness. We haven't created monsters. We aren't monsters. We want to be there for our children. You see so many people lose their young ones through suicide and they wonder why. This was why it was all the more important to be there for Shane.

(l. to r.) Graham, Shirley, Dennis and Shane

Out of the family closets

> *When I came out to Mum it was such a shock for her that I kept saying, 'It's okay, you're still my parents.'* **A gay son**

> *I had a desperate need to tell someone. I don't know why. I just felt I had to tell someone!* **A mum**

Parents tell me that three reactions may happen when their children first come out of the closet.

(l. to r.) Pam Garske, Narelle and Keith Phipps

1. 'Their coming out means I'm going into the closet'

> *When a child comes out, a parent lives the homophobia too. For example, they live the fear as a parent among their peers. And they may not have the energy to deal with stuff like that. But it's your child, and you should be able to tell your peers what they're doing if they're hurting your child and you.* **A mum**

Having an out GLBT child may at first appear to be something too hard to handle. Parents may find themselves glossing over or trivialising the life of their child when asked about him/her by other family members, friends and work colleagues. Evasions become common: 'there's no special girl in his life at the moment', 'she isn't thinking about marriage yet', 'he's sharing the apartment with a friend'.

Ask your children about closets. Remember, by the time your children come out to you, they will usually have had years of being closeted. They'll tell you being closeted requires an enormous amount of emotional and mental energy that interferes with personal and professional relationships. The cost of silence or deception takes its toll: remembering to be consistent with lies, juggling the different stories different people know, the explanations, the edits and erasures. If one good thing comes out of your experience of going into a closet, it will be an empathy with what your children and many in our society experience daily.

If your children want you to say something to some family members and friends, like I did, and you don't say anything, they feel that you're ashamed of them. That you're hiding it. For parents to say something to others tells their kids that everything's fine, they love them and it's no big deal. My parents tell everyone, but my partner's mum won't tell anyone. This means that if we go to her home or we go to family events, we're told explicitly not to look gay. It's not like that in my family because Mum is really open and tells every man and his dog. So we can be ourselves. **A daughter**

My mother-in-law is of the Queen Victoria school, that this wouldn't happen between women. When my daughter and her partner went to stay at her place interstate, she said, 'But of course you do realise there's only the double bed. That will be all right, won't it? You'll have to share the double bed.' My husband and I just stopped what we were doing. We looked at my daughter who said, 'Oh, okay.' I was trying so hard to keep a straight face, while my mother-in-law was totally oblivious to the whole thing. There's lots of things you can laugh about, but not being able to share it with people like your own parents is really difficult. **Anne**

It's about losing victimhood. No, this is not something that is a problem in my life. It's not something that is of major concern to me. It's a concern out there, it's a concern for a lot of other people, and I will not be a victim in this. **Barb**

2. 'Their coming to shore has set off tidal waves in my life'

I've broken off all contact with my family of origin because I couldn't cope with their comments that my daughter is a pervert. I said to them, 'No, what you people did to me and my daughter, that's the perversion.' We're now at the stage where they still keep sending me Christmas cards but don't accept my daughter. I let them know, 'I am not prepared to tolerate your homophobia or to deny my daughter's happiness just to satisfy your ignorance.' **A mum**

Some parents find that their child's coming out may have repercussions in other parts of their lives. So much of what may have lain dormant or buried in the sand now rises to the surface. For example, if you can't share the news with your partner or mother or friend or sibling, is this saying something about the kind of marriage, relationship, friendship you've always had that now comes to the fore and troubles you? Your child's coming out may raise old grievances and frustrations in other relationships and facets of your life that have never been resolved. Old frictions may be aggravated, new frictions added. Some parents may find themselves rethinking their own sexual histories and future, particularly if they have lived closeted GLBT lives.

If you and your partner are at very different points in responding to your child's coming out, conflict between you may arise or escalate. Thus, a child's coming out can have a negative effect on your relationship. For example, while one parent may need to go through some initial mourning period or lash out in anger and blame, the other is ready to affirm the child and support him/her against the outside world. With time, parents usually turn toward each other again, and often one parent assists the other in moving toward affirmation. Make sure that no matter what's happening between you and your partner, that you separate your own issues from those regarding your child. Reassure your child that they're not the cause of the fighting. Despite the tidal waves that you and your partner may need to swim and struggle through, make sure that your home remains a safe harbour for your child. Let them know that their other parent will get there too, it just may take longer for them to see the shore. And if your partner seems intent on drowning, let your child know that ultimately it's his/her choice and you and your child will not drown along with them.

Some parents may experience a positive effect in their relationship. They may feel more united as they join to shake the homophobic beliefs of other family members and the wider society.

Yes, some bonds will break, and some breakages will be permanent and painful. But some bonds will be strengthened, or superglued back together. Yes, fragile foundations may crumble, but strong foundations will become stronger, and new foundations will become possible.

My friend's ten years younger than me so her kids are a lot younger. I was baby-sitting one Saturday night a couple of years after Christopher had come out. Sarah was about twelve at the time, her brother ten, and the other two kids roughly the same age. A guy was chatting about another guy on TV and Sarah was coming down the stairs. She said, 'He's gay, he's going to kiss that photo, you watch. Oh, yuck.' I said, 'Oh, there's nothing wrong with being gay, Sarah.'

She went, 'Urk.'

Now, she loves and admires Christopher, so all I said was, 'Christopher's gay.'

'Oh.' No more. That was the end of the conversation.

On the Monday morning at work, my friend rang and said, 'Thanks for minding the kids on Saturday night but I've got a bone to pick with you.' I started laughing thinking, oh, right, I let the kids stay up too late. She said, 'You had no right to tell Sarah that Christopher was gay.'

This shook me for a little bit and I said, 'Oh, I think I did.'

'You had no right.'

'Robyn, I didn't go on about it. All I said was that comment. He's my son. Sarah said something negative, and I thought I'd just say something positive.'

'Well, we didn't think it was your position to do that. That would've been our position, to say it.'

Anyway, this blew all out of proportion. I felt really hurt. A couple of letters went backwards and forwards and unfortunately, after being close since she was nine years old, for the first time ever there was this rift.

But that was seven years ago. Just recently, Christopher went in a marching boys' squad and they had a rehearsal in a city street. Robyn came over with the video camera. So seven years ago she was obviously uncomfortable. She had young children. She probably just felt awkward about the whole thing. Perhaps she wasn't being rational. Perhaps I was being oversensitive as well. But what I feel is, set an example. **Katherine**

3. 'Their good feelings about themselves have made me have bad feelings about myself'

> *You sit there and think, 'Why is he doing this to me? I haven't done anything to him. I didn't deserve this. Why is he making my life so difficult?' You can be very selfish.* **A mum**

Some parents find that as their GLBT children let go of ugly feelings such as shame, guilt, grief, disappointment, self-blame, anger and despair, these very same feelings rise to the surface in themselves: 'I'm ashamed of my child', 'They won't have the life I'd dreamed for them', 'What did I do wrong?' 'This isn't fair, why my family?' 'I hate them for doing this to me', 'How do I hold my head up in the local church/town/community?' These feelings may often lead to further guilt, frustration and shame as 'good' parents are not meant to feel such things about their children. Thus, parents may block or 'closet' these reactions rather than working through them with their children, a counsellor and/or supportive friends.

Some parents feel 'bad' because this might be the first time they have ever experienced what it's like to be harassed or marginalised. Some white middle-class parents may have never experienced society's prejudices and attacks in any form before their children come out. Suddenly, they have gone from identifying as 'Mr and Mrs Average Citizen', comfortably part of the 'moral majority', to being a member of a minority group. They may never have developed the defences and resources to cope with rejection, discrimination and ostracism. Indeed, some parents may have participated in homophobic jokes and other prejudicial remarks themselves, and now find they experience guilt and shame when their own personal circumstances place them on the receiving end.

On the other hand, some parents may find that they don't feel guilty or frustrated or ashamed of their negative feelings toward their children. They are genuinely ashamed, angry, hateful and disappointed in their children and believe they have the right to be. That as 'good' parents, they deserved better from their children. Indeed, they may get angry if other parents or friends try to tell them these negative feelings are temporary or damaging in the long term.

> *Someone said to me very early in the piece, 'Aren't you lucky to have two gay children?' I was furious, absolutely furious! I didn't feel lucky at all about this 'terrible' thing that had happened to our family. Now, several years down the track, we just love being in communication with our children and their friends, and it has made us more tolerant and understanding, and me much less controlling!* **Gillian**

Onto the clothesline!

Remember that old saying, 'Don't hang your dirty washing on the clothesline for all to see!'

In this section, you're going to hear from some inspirational parents and families who refuse to treat their GLBT children as 'dirty washing'. They've supported, affirmed and celebrated their GLBT children coming out of dark suffocating closets to sun and air themselves on clotheslines – and yes, for all to see.

So what can parents do to work through the three reactions we've just talked about? How do you support yourself and in that way provide more effective support for your children?

Parents tell me the following six strategies are useful:

1. Find and create your own support and social networks.

> *When my daughter came out she had the gay community to go back to. They'd support her, but we didn't have support. My husband and I were floundering because we had no-one to talk to in our small country town. I'm not proud of the fact that I rejected her, but I didn't do it for long because you love your children.* **Margaret**

You may need formal and informal networks of other parents, family members, counsellors, community workers, trusted teachers and ministers with whom to ask questions, share fears and frustrations, share celebrations and good times. Keep in mind that the discussion of a child's sexuality must be approached with respect for the child's rights regarding who they want told or not told.

> *My father made a conscious effort to seek out people to talk to within the family. He actually told most of my relatives and they've been useful for him and also for me in making us closer. I've been invited to quite a number of family functions, and it always has 'To David and Friend' or 'David and Partner' on it. If your relatives are friendly and accepting, that can be useful to your parents.* **David**

> *I had PFLAG's number, but I wasn't game to ring it. I was saying, 'I'm not talking to the enemy. They're people who have two heads and will tell me to be happy that my daughter's gay. I'm not talking to anyone that's going to tell me that it's okay to be gay.' When you make that first phone call, or go to that first meeting, you may feel denial and grief and disgust and the whole circle of emotions, like feeling guilt that your child's gay. But you're going to reach out to a person that's going to listen to all that and there's no need to feel embarrassed. I cried so much at the first three meetings that people couldn't understand anything I said.* **Josie**

2. Replace a lifetime of ignorance, misinformation and prejudices with knowledge, awareness and understanding.

> *I think it's so sad that people get homosexuality and paedophilia confused, and that's where the big mistake is. Statistics show something like 80 percent of paedophiles are heterosexual males.* **Karen**

Both individually and with support networks, parents need to challenge social, cultural, political and religious myths and prejudices about sexual and gender diversity. Gather resources and connect with resource people to get informed with reliable facts. Open up a new way of speaking, seeing and experiencing a world that was always there, though you may have been prevented from seeing and understanding it by homophobic institutions and social forces.

> *My dad, Matthew's grandfather, said to me, 'You know, looking back now, there would've been a lot of gay guys in the armed forces with me but you just blanked it out. In my generation, you didn't talk about such things.'* **Elaine**

> *I realised how my own upbringing and Jewish background may have squashed communication with my daughter.* **Rose**

More and more young people are helping their parents become informed. They're getting information at school or at youth services, and going home with it to their families. Yes, young people are becoming the teachers, so ask your GLBT children for up-to-date information.

> *My son was very prepared. He said, 'This is who I am, and I don't feel guilty. There are support groups out there for you, there are books out there for you.' Then he said, 'Don't ask any more questions because you just have to settle,' as I'd started with one million questions. Two days later, we were in the gay parts of town buying books and getting to know more.* **A mum**

> *It's nice to get all that information.* **A dad**

> *Do some reading yourself so you can understand what your parents are going through, even if it's as clinical as having a list of things you need to teach your parents or explain to your parents. They might burst into flames but over the next few months, work with them, encourage them to talk through their issues.* **Alan**

So, if you're a GLBT young person or a sibling of a GLBT young person reading this – here's your chance to set your parents homework!

> *Before I came out, I read a whole stack of books to find out a lot more and also to prepare myself for the questions that were going to come from my parents. Then when I came out to my parents, I just said, 'Read these.' Yeah, like, 'Here's your homework.'* **James**

3. Work through a range of reactions and feelings such as anger, hurt, frustration, disappointment, shame, blame of self and others.

> *The main thing is reassure your kids that you love them and if you're not dealing with it, it's your trouble, that you'll work it out. That even though you don't know what to do, you'll try, you'll try. I said, 'I still love you. I'm not coping with this, but I'm going to try, and we'll work it out.' Six months it took me. I think we need to keep going through everyday life with our kids, together, and meanwhile keep working at it.* **A dad**

Now, I don't mean to sound harsh here, but remember, you are the parent and with that comes a parent's love, responsibility and accountability to your children. Your role is to lighten their load, to love them, to provide them with a sense of safety and security when they're at home. Make sure that in coming out, your children aren't prevented from coming home. And yes, learn how to stay strong together against the unfortunately inevitable buffeting storms that will come from the world outside your home.

My daughter was very patient with us and kept loving us, knowing how religious we are. She is quite religious too so it was an issue that affected her and affected us. **A mum**

I rang this friend who was gay, and told her my daughter had come out. She said, 'That's fantastic,' and was really excited. So that was really good for me to hear, to have someone react that way. She also said, 'The first things that you say will be what she remembers, how you say it will be remembered, and one day she'll be able to tell you what you said to her.' This friend said that her partner can remember her dad's exact words: 'Oh, nothing could be worse, you're one of those.' So when I talked to my daughter about it, I went into her room, sat on the floor so I wasn't taller than her, and we had a discussion about it rather than me abusing her. **A mum**

When you come out to your parents, the basic thing you want to hear is they still love you and will stick by you. You don't expect them to be perfect or understand it all, but that they're willing to work it all out. **A daughter**

Lighten the load your GLBT children may be carrying in the bigger world with laughter and humour at home! Affirming and affectionate humour is a great healer.

Daughter: I think laughter is so healthy. For example, when all the gay members of my family came out, my mum decided, 'Okay, I'm straight, so I'm the minority.'

Mum: Yes, I'm the butt of all the jokes in my family.

Daughter: And what's it like being in a minority, Mum?

Mum: A real pain. They pick on you, they stir you. Oh, it's shocking.

My dad actually said, 'Now we have something in common ... we both like breasts!' **Dianne**

4. Come in to their coming out.

Let your kids talk about what's important to them, what's worrying them, what it's been like for them. **A dad**

Listen to and chat with your children about the past, the present, and how they would like you to support them in the future. Become involved in your children's coming out processes, according to their wishes. It's important that young people are in control of: when they come out; who they come out to; and how they come out. Keeping that in mind, and respecting their wishes, you can facilitate in many ways. Coming out is not an outcome or single event. It occurs every time a GLBT person shares information about their sexuality with another person. The coming out process can be complicated. Check out the 'Coming out' checklist on page 37 with your child. Remember, this constant coming out and emotional negotiation is something heterosexual young people do not have to experience. Reassure them that you understand coming out is forced upon them by an ignorant society, that it's not a reflection of their sexuality being a deficiency or freakish state.

Many GLBT young people are afraid to come out as they fear losing their role in a family they love. Reassure them that they're still loved and lovable members of the family, and that their loving of others in the family is still important.

My son and I had to revisit a lot of things that had happened, or had been confusing, or never been explained. It was like sitting down and going, 'So you know when that happened, is that because of this?' It was really like another growth for both of us. It was like a sharing together, a journey together, reconnecting and healing old wounds that you sometimes didn't even know had been there. Some parents will say their kids' coming out is the end, a crisis, and feel like there's nowhere to go from here. That's a shame because it can be a new beginning, to get over past mistakes. **A mum**

Pity

Tolerance

Acceptance

5. Script, stage and manage your own frequent outings about being the parents of a GLBT child.

> *If we don't come out about gay family members, homosexuality will always be suppressed, because people that you work with or your neighbours or family may not knowingly know anybody who's GLBT. They never have any everyday role models except what they see on TV.* **Karen**

Coming out about your child's coming out means standing up against the homophobia that still prevails in society. This involves facing your own inner fears and doubts about your child and yourself, and facing the reactions of those around you. Each time you tell another person, you take a step away from your own prejudice, help the other person take a step away from their own prejudice, and with these steps you're helping society shift!

Your outings may differ according to who it is you're coming out to. As your children will tell you, there's no coming out medicine ready to be stirred and taken by all. Again, check out the 'Coming out' checklist on page 37 and apply it to your coming outs.

> *Practise some responses you'll make if people ask you things.* **A mum**

> *About a year after my son had come out, I'd gained more confidence, and I actually did want to go around standing on a soapbox and saying that I was very proud. He and his friends were coming back from a holiday and I was meeting him at the airport. I had a rainbow bracelet on, a rainbow necklace and I can't remember what else. He got off the plane, just looked at me, and then said, 'Jesus, Mum, you look like a dyke.'* **Karen**

As parents, you'll be trying to support and care for everyone in the family, and taking into account everyone's needs and situations, not just your GLBT child's needs. It's really important to be as out as possible, but it's okay to be careful who you come out to, especially if you have younger children, especially if they're still at school and likely to be bullied, and especially if you're living in a neighbourhood or area where your family may experience harm.

> *We'd like to do more public work but when we ask the younger kids in the family, 'Would you like us to do the TV show, would you be comfortable with that?' there's fear on the faces of the little ones and the 'I don't want anyone at school to know that she's gay'. So I have to always take into account what they feel. We put it to a family vote, and I have to respect them as well because they're growing up too. And we have had graffiti and stuff thrown at our house already.* **Josie**

6. Be proud of your children – don't pedestal them or punish them.

> *I was at a dinner party with colleagues and relatives. Everyone was talking about their daughters' weddings, engagements and asking about each other's children. But no one asked me about my daughter. So I started talking about my daughter's achievements and about her relationship. I wasn't going to be silenced or made to feel ashamed. I wanted to show how proud I was of her.* **Rose**

Coming out to you has required tremendous energy, strength, trust and love. It's also saying something incredibly positive and beautiful about what you have with your child, how important you are to your child. Be proud of that as well. Whatever you're feeling, affirm and reassure, and honour their love, trust and strength.

> *Two o'clock in the morning with my son after an evening out with my son and his friends, getting a hamburger, wandering home through the park arm in arm. He's been our greatest teacher.* **Shirley**

32

Don't 'pedestal' your children: they won't be perfect in other ways just to compensate for being GLBT. Like all kids, they will make mistakes and have aspects of themselves you may not always like. This is not because they are GLBT but because they're human. Don't see everything they do through what's known as 'the master signifier' or the 'tunnel vision lens', that their being GLBT is the reason or justification for everything they say or do. By the way, some people will now see you only through the 'tunnel vision' lens of 'parent of gay child'.

Don't 'punish' your children: being GLBT is not a bad thing, even if society out there says it is. Remember, only a few decades ago, there was so much criminalising and pathologising of same-sex attraction and gender diversity. Prisons or hospitals were the places for all that 'deviance'. There have been legal and social changes, but not enough. You have a big part to play in making it even easier for generations that come after your children by the way you do your bit to make your own children's lives easier, loving and healthy.

> We hardly need to educate the young kids in our family about my son being gay. They're seeing so much of it on TV and in films and the media. All the youngest kids and my nieces and grandkids say, 'Big deal, what's the big deal?' They're fine with my son. **Michelle**

By the way, as our children remind us, parents make mistakes too! You are a parent but you're still human so don't punish or 'pedestal' yourself either. Sometimes you will make mistakes or not handle things the way 'good parents should'. That's okay as long as you backtrack soon after, apologise to your child, and move forward in more productive ways.

Rudy and Mary are two strong and inspirational parents whose son came out after he got married. Their honest account of their experiences reminds us to encourage openness and love when our children are young, to provide a home free of homophobic put-downs and behaviours, so that years of torment, loneliness and pretence that may also hurt other people, can be avoided.

I think everybody should have a gay child
Rudy and Mary Vanderhart

Mary: It all started when I rang my daughter-in-law. My son was overseas an awful lot, and when I rang her, she was crying. I said, 'What's the matter?' She said, 'No, no, no, I can't tell you.'

I said, 'Why can't you tell me?'

'Well, Glen has to tell you.'

I was getting worried, so I rang her mother, 'What's wrong with Yvonne? Has she lost a baby, what's wrong?'

She said, 'No, it's not Yvonne, it's Glen.'

'Has he had an accident?'

'No, no. I can't really tell you because he wants to tell you himself.'

I asked, 'Are they going to get separated? Has he got another girlfriend?'

'No.'

'Has he got a boyfriend?'

And she said, 'You said it.'

That's how it started. Then Glen rang us because he wanted to tell us himself.

Rudy: It was me who picked up the phone. I can't remember what I said, but all I know is that he started to cry and I started to cry. I wanted to say so much but couldn't because there was a lot of pain involved. So Mary took the phone and had a conversation with him. It was the biggest shock of my life, because to me, it was unexpected.

I had come home that day and Mary was sitting in the lounge. She said, 'You better sit down and have a Scotch.' It was the biggest Scotch I've ever seen. She told me that she'd found out that Glen was gay. It was very, very hurtful, very devastating. I could feel the pain he must've felt all those years, listening to me, his homophobic father. I'd made a lot of stupid remarks, not knowing that I had a gay child, and that hurt me the most, really. 'Put all the gays on an island and throw the key away,' all those stupid things. At that time, you probably reckon it's smart, but looking back on it, it must've really hurt him. And that was the hurt I was feeling now.

Mary: Glen told me he'd known he was gay since he was eight years old. I thought he must've been living a very lonely life in his teenage years. He couldn't talk to anybody. There was nobody there for him. If he could've told us, even in his teenage years, he would never have gotten married in the first place. Now he felt he was living a lie and with stupid homophobic remarks we made as a family, he felt he had to keep on lying. He was thinking he could live a lie for the rest of his life. But now that he was coming out to us, there was also a sense of relief among all the hurt.

Rudy: After that day, we often rang Glen where he lived in Las Vegas and then we went for six weeks to see him, his partner and his partner's parents. That was a relief for myself too, because I could say I was sorry about my stupid behaviour and lack of knowledge.

Mary: Our upbringing was so old fashioned. I remember an experience one night when we were with my son in Las Vegas. I said to Glen, 'I'm going to bed,' but soon after I went downstairs to get a Coke. I was in the kitchen and the boys were in the pool, passionately kissing each other. I told myself, 'Yeah, that's normal for them, that is absolutely normal.' I had to talk to myself. And now if they do it, it doesn't hurt me any more.

It was hard for Rudy to be open with family and friends. One day we had the neighbours over for a cup of tea and they asked how the kids were going. I said, 'Oh, Glen is gay and he lives in Las Vegas.'

Rudy nearly fell off his chair. He said, 'You're not going to sit there and say that our daughter is heterosexual, so why tell people Glen is gay? It has nothing to do with them.'

I said, 'I feel that if I can tell everybody, then it's off my chest and they have to accept it the way it is. If they accept him, then they accept me. They have to accept my son.'

You'd be surprised how, if you talk to people about someone being gay in your family, they all have somebody in their family who's gay! One time, just after the Sydney Gay and Lesbian Mardi Gras, I was walking the dogs around the lake in the park and I met this woman. We started talking and I said, 'Oh, look at the rainbow. It makes me think of the Mardi Gras.'

She said, 'Did you go?'

I said, 'I've got a gay son.'

And she said, 'So do I.'

Rudy: At first, I never could see any value in talking about somebody's sex life. At work, I told some fellows that I have a gay son and they were very understanding. I'm very careful about who I tell because there are certain religious groups you can't talk to because they've got a one-track mind and they just don't want to listen. I'm sure the time will come that they'll change, because everything has changed over the last one hundred years.

Mary: I talked to my nine-year-old granddaughter about Uncle Glen getting married to Uncle Les. I sat down and explained, 'Not everybody's the same, and this is something schools and society don't talk about. Uncle Glen loves Uncle Les so they got married and a lot of women get married to each other because they love each other.'

Our lives are much richer now. We've learnt so much. We don't live in the little square box any more. We can appreciate different lifestyles. People are not made from the same moulds.

I think everybody should have a gay child and then the homophobia would be totally gone. Because if you love your children, that's all that matters.

Rudy: What Mary's said is so true. You appreciate other people more and you just accept them as they are. Some people are kinky, happy, gay, heterosexual, it doesn't matter. Don't kick your kids out. Talk to them. Love them.

(l. to r.) Les, Glen, Mary and Rudy

Coming out: a checklist

This checklist can be used by:

▶▶ young people coming out

▶▶ parents assisting their children to come out

▶▶ parents in their own coming out about their children's coming out.

▶▶ **Why do I want to come out? Am I feeling pressured by others or threatened?**
'Because I'm proud of who I am', ' I want them to know so we can have a better relationship', and 'I'm proud of who my children are' are great reasons.

▶▶ **What do I know about being gay/lesbian/bisexual/transgender?**
'Will I be able to answer questions?' Doing some reading, talking to a trusted counsellor, teacher, youth worker, phone line, accessing info on the web, talking to a PFLAG parent, will all prepare you for the kinds of stereotypes and ignorant assumptions/questions some people might have.

▶▶ **What attitude do the people I want to tell seem to have toward GLBT people?**
Test possible reactions by telling them about someone else, asking them about something on TV or the news, setting up a chat or meeting with another parent who just 'happens' to have a GLBT child.

▶▶ **What's the mood of the situation?**
Choose when to tell. Try not to tell people during an argument or to use the issue as a weapon. This may distance people and catch them when they're already feeling aggressive, defensive or overly sensitive.

▶▶ **Can I be patient?**
People often require time to deal with the information. Can you give them time to adjust and to understand? Can you hang in there while they get over the initial shock?

▶▶ **How strong do I feel?**
What helps you feel strong? Is now a good time to come out, or should you wait till you feel stronger? Do you want someone there with you? A counsellor? Teacher? Youth worker? A friend?

▶▶ **Can I trust the people I'm going to tell not to tell others unless I want them to?**

How will you maintain control over this? How will you talk about this with the person? What do you know about how they have handled similar situations of confidentiality and trust in the past?

▶▶ **How much support do I have?**

'Am I prepared if I'm rejected?' Do you have physical, financial and emotional resources should things go bad? If you are a young GLBT person and you think you'll be rejected at home, make sure you have back-up resources like a plan to stay at someone else's house, and someone to speak to afterward.

▶▶ **How will I come out?**

Talking openly, writing a letter or email, telephoning, asking a sibling or friend to tell them, telling your parent to tell others?

▶▶ **Is it safe to come out?**

The most important question! If your life or family's life is threatened, find a youth worker or helpline and talk it through. If a situation could potentially be unsafe, what will you need in order to work through it or remove yourself from it?

Members of the Yellowkitties social and support group for lesbians of Asian backgrounds

Test the waters
The YGLAM Youth Group

— Test the water a little bit. There's one little trick I used to do. I would come up to someone and say, 'Oh, a friend of mine just came out to me,' and start talking about it. I would then just gauge their reaction and if they were okay, I'd actually change the situation around and talk about me.

— Know what your family feels about other controversial subjects and issues, and if they've had any personal experiences of differences, how they react to it. If they believe in traditional gender roles and always believe there's a right and wrong way of being a male and female, they're likely to have issues with being gay.

— When I told my mum, I thought we were very close and I was expecting that whole hug, 'I love you anyway' thing. I didn't get it. I didn't get it for about a year and it took that year for my mum to actually come to terms with it. So that's advice I'd give young people – don't be too disheartened if at first it doesn't look like a good reaction because over time things will probably get better.

GLBT young people come from many different kinds of families, such as ethnic families, each with a heritage of cultural and religious traditions, values, beliefs and expectations. These will include differing ideas, information and values regarding same-sex attraction and gender diversity. Our children should be supported to live comfortably and happily in many worlds, rather than feel like they have to choose between their ethnic family and heritage and being GLBT. Let's remember that our cultures are not only what we inherit but what we make of what we inherit. Cultures don't stay the same, they're constantly changing, and making our cultures support and celebrate GLBT members is culture-enhancing.

> *My parents are staunch Greek Orthodox and traditional, almost stereotypical 'old country'. We've spoken on occasion, my parents telling me that although they'll always view it as unnatural, they are there for me if ever I need them.* **Vicky**

Have a listen to three young women of different Asian backgrounds who are part of a social and support group called Yellowkitties. They talk about their families and their sexualities, and their desire to honour both.

'My family is so important to me': Yellowkitties talk coming out

Charmaine: I've never actually sat down and said to my parents 'I'm a lesbian'. But I think my parents know because I'm quite close to them. When I was living at home, I had my girlfriends come over and my parents never really said anything, they never even made an issue. It's something that's not discussed, but something that they know exists. And I guess that sort of keeps the peace. But my mum has asked me, 'Do you prefer the company of a lady?'

It's important for my partners to know my family. I don't know if it's an ethnic Indian thing whereby it seems that women loving women is quite acceptable. I don't know what it would be like if my brother were to come out.

T: But when you say 'come out' do you mean 'come out' in a formal Western way? My parents are Japanese. My mum used to own a hostess bar and she's been through a lot. She's seen all sorts of women. But usually in Japanese culture, many Japanese lesbians are not out, not even to their friends, partly because articulation is not that important. By saying that you're a lesbian, that would ruin the whole thing – like family structure, or community unity. So the silence is coming from fear and discrimination, but also from the fact that in our culture, there's not that much emphasis on needing to verbalise and articulate everything.

Charmaine: I know my Anglo lesbian friends always say to me, 'You've gotta tell your parents, you've gotta tell your parents.' They feel that my parents know anyway because whenever I'd have a party, I'd have about fifteen women there, and a lot of them look like men, and my parents treat them really well. My parents got to know my last girlfriend, who I'd been with for a long while. And even now they call her over for dinner, even when I'm not there. So I think it's sort of unspoken, but I know they're not stupid.

Lian: Yeah. There's still a lot of stigma talking about it in the Malaysian community, or acknowledging you being a lesbian, but they may accept it because you're part of the family.

Charmaine: Well I remember my grandmother always said, 'Charmaine, never let a boy see your *susu* [genitalia].' And so I just listened to my grandma!

T: Does she have a very traditional Indian background?

Charmaine: Yup. My girlfriends have met her too. I don't know what she knows but you know she knows. And like my parents, it's about me being happy. So they've sort of come to that conclusion that if I'm happy then that's all that matters. And even now, when my girlfriend and I went to visit my mum, she said to me, 'Where are you sleeping?' I didn't say anything but we just put all our stuff in the guest room with the double bed. And we stayed there for two weeks. We had an en suite and everything. It means so much to me because my family is so important to me. Obviously I'm important to them too. If they did have a hard time, I'd have a really hard time.

Lian: I came out when I was about eighteen but I always kind of knew. I was living with my parents and I shaved my head and all that. But the way I came out was always through writing stuff. I had to come out to them the day before my dad's birthday because there was a very personal monologue that I wrote for a public playwriting competition, so it was something that I had to tell them. My parents, my brother, my grandmother, and my uncle were all there. And that was all right. But I don't know if it was something they totally understand. My mum's very supportive, but with my dad there's still issues.

Charmaine: I don't know about you, but the whole idea and prospect of coming out was so daunting because my parents raised us as you raise your daughters in India, being very protective. I was never allowed to go out or sleep at someone's house till I was eighteen. As it turns out, it's been easier for me than some of my Anglo friends who got kicked out of home and stuff like that.

Lian: That was what I was afraid of. I actually got this idea that they'd be so upset with me that they'd kick me out of home.

Charmaine: Yeah, because you hear these stories about these things happening, and you think, 'Oh my god, if that was in a white family, who should be more hip to stuff, what about my family? How would they react?'

T: In Japan it's much harsher. Many lesbians or gay guys are not out to their families. I think I'm one of the generation's few out young Japanese lesbians. And I didn't want to come out. My mum just found me kissing a girl in my bedroom when I was fourteen. My mum just closed the door and left us alone. But I had to come out twice. Because she thought that was a growing-up phase. She occasionally asked me if I had a boyfriend, so I formally came out two years ago. And I was on TV too, broadcast in Japan!

Lian: I'm very comfortable about being a lesbian. When my grandmother was here from Malyasia, I felt like I couldn't say all of who I am as a lesbian, about my lesbian friends and everything. I felt like I had to suppress all that. She was asking me, 'When are you getting married?'

Charmaine: I don't know if it's similar in your cultures but there's very traditional Indian stuff about marrying off your daughters and getting the dowry, so tradition is really centred on that. That's why I was worried about my parents' reaction.

Lian: Yup, because of their background. My grandma makes comparisons, like when she was my age, she was already married. Some of my parents' friends' children about my age are getting married.

T: Yeah, marriage is such a big deal. Especially for women in our cultures.

Charmaine: Within the Japanese culture too?

T: Oh, of course, of course. Once you're in your twenties, people talk about marriage.

Charmaine: My grandmother was thirteen when she married her husband, who was 30. And it was obviously arranged. I think she was sixteen when she had her first child. My parents weren't an arranged marriage. I think maybe in that generation it stopped. Some of my parents' friend's were arranged. Marrying off your daughter when you're really young can't happen when you move to a Western country.

T: Both of my parents are in Japan. They still have the cultural ways of thinking. But my family is very atypical. Like my mum being older than my dad, and my mum used to earn much more than my dad did.

Lian: Did that make an impact on you growing up, that your mother was a very strong independent woman?

T: Well she was definitely a strong influence on me. Because of her business, the owner of a hostess bar, where she accommodated many kinds of women, those who suffered from domestic violence to ex-housewives. If they break up with their husbands, there's nowhere to go, and many of these women had no employable skills. So what they go for is usually hostessing, for my mother's generation anyway. She once had this really butch woman working at the counter. And because of that she's had connections with the gay community as well. So she's had lesbian friends. But she did have trouble with her own daughter being a lesbian because I'm an only child and being a lesbian means being infertile in her mind. That means stopping the future of the family basically. My parents are feeling insecure even now because I'm living overseas and I'm everything they have. And I need to inherit their house.

Lian: Yeah, that family pressure, that kind of responsibility. You've got to carry on the family name.

T: Family responsibility, yes. Apparently in Japan, I guess in India and in Malaysia as well, family obligations are much stronger than in Western countries, where there are more individualistic values and more independence from your family.

Charmaine: I see it like that too. I know in my parents' community there's no divorce because it's a big shame. I know it's an antiquated way of thinking but it's still a big deal.

Ten common questions parents ask ... and more than ten easy answers to support you support your child!

1. 'Why did they choose to be homosexual?'

After our son came out, my husband said, 'I always knew in my heart.' I asked him why he'd always been so homophobic then, and he said, 'Well, I was just letting him know if you have a choice, don't choose that.' But I'm not here to actually investigate if it's genes or choice. It doesn't make any difference. **Karla**

To date, no-one knows what determines sexuality. The theories out there are unfortunately still couched in that 'nature versus nurture' boxing ring. While research is underway, what matters is that your child *is*, and that child needs love and care, affirmation and celebration. Reducing your child to a research subject or a case study in working out what made them 'like that' is far less important than getting on with what matters – life, love, connection.

Some parents feel that the child has chosen to be homosexual as an act of rebellion. No-one 'chooses' to be homosexual unless they have same-sex desires. Most people say they have known all their lives they are GLBT, others work through shifting feelings and desires. Some people may see it as a trend within some youth cultures, but the trend

Photo courtesy of Sam Trigg

passes unless the person feels something inside. Again, sexuality can shift and/or remain fixed over the course of a lifetime, and what's written off as 'choice of sexuality' is a person choosing to follow their inner same-sex desires and attractions rather than continuing to regulate and repress them according to social expectations. So, of course, as society becomes more

45

understanding and informed about sexual and gender diversity, more young people will feel able to come out or try out different sexualities and genders rather than pretend to be heterosexual or rigidly male/female. Thus, when you hear someone spouting out that 'today's sexual permissiveness promotes homosexuality' and that 'talking about homosexuality is about recruiting young people to that lifestyle', you can reply, 'Increasing social and scientific awareness and affirmation of sexual diversity and gender diversity promotes a healthy self-awareness and self-confidence in young people. They can be whatever sexuality and do their gender in any way that feels good for them.'

> Unfortunately, some gay people make a conscious decision to try to live a heterosexual life and then find that's unnatural for them. Or some bisexual people try to live a gay or straight life and find that's unnatural for them. And some transgender people decide to slot into what society defines as 'male' or 'female'. But they're all forced into a devastating decision. I don't call that choice. That's coercion! **Naomi**

Sexual orientation and attractions are part of our whole being, interwoven with our ongoing lives and the people we meet. Sexual identity is not an out-of-the-blue conscious decision. Do heterosexual people remember a time when they made a conscious decision to be attracted to the opposite sex? No? It wasn't a decision, it just 'was', fostered and nurtured by the celebratory and approving responses and encouragement of everyone and everything around you. And because people assume heterosexuality is the 'normal natural' way, then anything else is seen by some as a conscious decision to be otherwise.

> One thing I often say to students when I'm giving a talk about being a mother of a gay son is, 'When did you decide to be straight?' and they can't answer that. And I say, 'It's the same for gay people.' I tell them about my childhood: 'I'm attracted to males. I guess it was just a natural thing from when I was little and used to play Kiss Chasey. I was always attracted to Jim. Jane never entered the picture.' **Karen**

2. 'Where did we go wrong?'

A son: When I first told my dad, he said, 'Oh, is it something we've done? Is it because you didn't play enough sport?'

A dad: That's a classic for some dads like me. When my son came out, I thought, 'I should've made him play football instead of allowing him to go to drama classes. I should've made him mow the lawns.'

Many parents feel guilty that their child is GLBT, as if they are in some way to 'blame'. No-one is at fault. There is no fault to be allocated because there's nothing wrong with being GLBT. Do we hear people asking: 'what makes children heterosexual'?

Simple questions to ask yourself about your own sexuality when doubt floods in or when others try and make you feel your GLBT child is a product of 'bad' parenting:

▶▶ When did you first know you were straight?

▶▶ What made you straight?

▶▶ What did your family do that's made you straight even though you know you were meant to be gay?

Do these questions seem nonsensical or unanswerable in relation to heterosexuality? Then why do we think it's 'normal' to apply them in relation to homosexuality, bisexuality and gender diversity?

What makes us feel that we've done something 'wrong' if our children are GLBT? It's unfortunate that many of the early studies that were done with GLBT people and their families were undertaken with clients of counsellors or those seeking therapy and medical intervention for this 'sexuality problem', rather than researching with happy and healthy families of happy and healthy GLBT people. And of course, research reflected the dominant psychiatric and psychological view that being GLBT was an illness or deficit anyway, so all the more reason to find its 'cause' and 'cure'.

We often hear from the medical profession and counselling services that the way a child turns out is the parents' responsibility. Certainly, upbringing and home environment have a major role to play in children's behaviour, attitudes and values, and health and wellbeing, in relation to their sexuality. This is all the more reason why we need to think carefully about the kind of home environment a GLBT young person has been raised in, and what we can provide now for our children. Maybe the home environment made it harder for our children to feel comfortable and affirmed in their sexuality and gender because we tried so hard to fit them into normative social grooves about what it means to be 'male' and 'female', and how important it is to develop a 'normal heterosexual' sexuality.

Think about the social regulations and gendered assumptions that underlie the following common 'blame/cause' statements and questions:

▶▶ You were too protective with your son.

▶▶ You let your daughter run around like a boy.

▶▶ As a mum you were too involved with your son.

▶▶ As a mum you weren't involved enough with your daughter.

▶▶ As a dad you were too absent from your son.

▶▶ As a dad you were too present with your daughter.

▶▶ Did you hug your son too much and allow him to cry too much?

▶▶ Was your daughter allowed to play with 'boys' toys?

▶▶ Should you have made your daughter wear dresses?

▶▶ You shouldn't have given your son that teddy bear and allowed him to take it everywhere.

▶▶ Did you encourage normal feminine and masculine pursuits and behaviour?

The very fact that these statements and questions come up reveals how the surface of the gender and sexual tapestry is so rigid and unhealthy in our society. If you look at the underside of that tapestry, there are so many people in knots and tangles that eat away at hearts and souls, the legacy of an upbringing of being made to conform. Isn't there something 'wrong' with that?

Make sure your resources are up to date. I remember when my father found out I was gay. He went to the encyclopaedia, which was published like in the 1900s. And the first thing he said was, 'Did I mother you too much? Is it my fault? Wasn't I there enough for you?' **Peter**

My mum found it difficult to accept that my sexuality was not 'caused' by previous events in my life. I was raped and I had to deal with the trauma of not feeling safe, of fear, depression and deep psychological scarring as a result. My mother blames these attacks for my sexuality, a view underscoring the opinion of homosexuality being a disease that is treatable by professionals. **Patricia**

3. 'Could this be just a phase? Are they sure? How do they know?'

> *My father said, 'You're too young and immature to know what sexuality is, let alone know that you're gay.'* **Tania**

Sometimes it is a phase, most of the time it isn't. This kind of question is also based on another social myth, that sexuality is clean-cut and fixed for life. For many people, this isn't so. Sexual desires may shift and flux throughout a lifetime. Heterosexuality has often proved to be the phase. Heterosexuality has often been the enforced sexuality against which same-sex attraction struggles and eventually comes through. Do we ask heterosexual-identifying children: 'Could this just be a phase? Are you sure? How do you know?' Don't we accept, indeed encourage, that heterosexual-identifying children 'know' their sexuality at a very young age, laughing at their early childhood flirtations and enjoying their playground 'boyfriend/girlfriend' pairings? So why do we then assume that same-sex attracted children are too young, too immature to 'know' their sexuality?

It shouldn't matter whether same-sex attraction lasts a week, a month, a year, decades, a lifetime. It's about acknowledging and respecting the feelings of the young person *at the time*, making it okay for children to be whatever sexuality they are or will be. It's about providing skills of communication about one's sexual desires and skills of negotiation with others in order to be able to enter relationships with honesty and openness about one's desires. Again, the problem is not one's sexuality, in its fixed lifelong or shifting forms, but the social restrictions and silences that prevent people from being open, honest and loving in the way they work through these issues.

49

> *When my son's school counsellor tried to reassure me that this was a phase he was going through and that he'd soon be normal, I turned it around and said, 'And is this a phase you're going through? Do you think you might need some counselling on what's normal and what isn't?'* **Mario**

Bisexual young people are often told they're going through a phase, and this comes not only from straight homophobes but from gay or lesbian biphobes! If a bisexual young person talks about 'feeling confused', it's because they lack support and affirmation of their sexuality. Bisexuality is not confusing. Society and certain groups within the gay community still stuck in the either/or model create the confusion. They marginalise bisexual people, or make them invisible by calling them gay if they're in a same-sex relationship, or straight if they're in an opposite-sex relationship.

4. 'Homosexual relationships are purely based on sex. They don't last.'

> *Very rarely will the relationships of your gay children ever be mentioned, and for a parent that's very hurtful. Whatever the sexuality, a relationship is a relationship, and a loving relationship should be acknowledged by people. Our first son has been in a straight relationship for seven years. His partner is regarded by all the extended family as part of the family. But there's not the same degree of acceptance for our second son and his partner.* **Warren**

All human beings want and need someone or a group of people to share their lives with based on attraction, love, caring and sharing. Sex is part of everyone's life, whatever their sexuality or gender. Some heterosexuals have relationships purely based on sex too. Casual flings and one-night stands are casual flings and one-night stands, no matter what the sexuality.

There's as much diversity in sexual patterns among GLBT people as there is among straight people.

Society has made it pretty tough for many GLBT people to establish and maintain long-term relationships. Look at the failure rate of heterosexual relationships despite all the political, legal, religious, social, institutional and cultural props! Imagine wanting to hold hands on a street and you can't. Imagine wanting to have an argument and then kiss and make up in a supermarket or a park, and you can't. Instead, you have all that emotional seething building up till you get home to work it out in a private space. I always finds it ironic that those who deny GLBT people's right to have publicly acknowledged, celebrated and affirmed relationships are the ones who say these relationships are just about sex, or they don't last.

In my family, it's all right that I'm gay, but they don't want to talk about my relationship, they don't want to hear about it. I challenge them all, 'Well, why not? I hear about your straight partner. I hear about your wife. I'm going to tell you about my partner.' They tell me their relationships are normal and they ask me why I have to talk about my partner all the time. 'Well, you know, you talk about your wife or your husband or your children all the time. I'm talking about my family.' **Paul**

When my son Kieran and his partner Tim had a commitment ceremony, we did the whole thing. We had a proper reception, we had flowers and we sent out invitations. I had a lovely outfit to wear and went to the hairdresser, got my hair all boofed up, and did all the things that I'd done the year before when our daughter was married. It was a beautiful celebration, but somebody said to me, 'They haven't really known each other very long. How long is this going to last?' So, I pointed out to the person that the period of time in which they had known each other was the same as the period of time in which John and I had known each other before we were married, and we've got 40 years coming up this year. So, hopefully Kieran and Tim will celebrate their Ruby Anniversary. **Nan**

One issue that's being increasingly addressed openly and honestly is the diversity of ways relationships can be organised and structured. For example, they can be non-monogamous as well as monogamous. As GLBT people have not had their relationships structured and regulated by social, religious and cultural codes as much as heterosexual relationships, many GLBT people have explored various ways of negotiating long-term relationships. And if this is constructed as indicative of 'sexual promiscuity', we need only consider the amount of secretive extramarital sex that happens in heterosexual relationships that officially endorse monogamy and are institutionally defined as monogamous!

My son's bisexual and has been in a relationship with a woman and a man for over ten years. They now have a child. Some bisexuals are monogamous, as are some straights and gays. Some people, no matter what their sexuality, are polyamorous. They can love more than one person at a time. What matters is that there is genuine love and honest communication and negotiation. This is much healthier than trying to squeeze into a monogamous marriage that doesn't work for many straights anyway. **Naomi**

5. 'Why do they have to flaunt their sexuality in public?'

A friend of mine was very loving towards both of his nephews, the hetero-sexual one and the homosexual one, and they were all at the beach one day. The heterosexual one was putting suntan lotion on the shoulders of his girlfriend. And it was very normal, the kind of thing that young, courting couples do. The uncle was talking to the gay nephew, 'Well, the problem with gays is why do they always have to flaunt it?' He thought they were flaunting their sexuality because he'd been uncomfortable when the gay nephew had wanted to run into the surf holding hands with his boyfriend. The nephew's comment was, 'What's my brother and his girlfriend doing? They're flaunting their sexuality on the beach with the suntan oil. If I was to bring my boyfriend over here and he was to lie down, and I was to put suntan oil on his back, would that be flaunting? But that's what they're doing.' And it was my friend who told me this story, the classic example of the distinctions we make between what's normal, what's acceptable, and what's not. I think that you have to have those close encounters with reality before your brain opens up to the possibility that you're discriminating in ways you just weren't aware of. **Geoffrey**

Often parents and other family members feel uncomfortable with open displays of affection by their GLBT children toward their partners. We only feel this way because society has made it hard for GLBT people to be affectionate and demonstrative in public, and so we're not used to seeing it. Unless they are part of so-called lesbian sex for straight male viewing in porn. That's considered 'normal'! Let's ask ourselves: are we consistent in what we define as 'flaunting' sexuality? Do we feel the same about heterosexual displays of affection? Why shouldn't GLBT young people be able to show that they love and care for someone, just as heterosexuals do? This is our problem, not our children's, and we have to learn to deal with it. We need to see their affection toward their partners as positive, healthy and beautiful, not negative, sick and deviant. And your children may wish and need to express their love and desires openly in the home because it's so hard to express it in public.

Dad 1: A lot of parents don't even like seeing them holding hands, touching each other, kissing. So it's a big hurdle that many parents have to overcome.

Mum 1: We have to overcome that with our heterosexual children too. My son just drives me mad, he and his girlfriend, wow!

Dad 2: Our daughter doesn't have a girlfriend yet. But when she actually gets that first serious sexual relationship, how am I going to cope? That's my biggest worry.

Mum 2: You tell yourself they're expressing how they love each other.

Dad 2: Yes, I know. I'll have to deal with it. My only worry is I may react badly to it. I'm hoping I won't.

Dad 1: It's just that we're not used to seeing it.

Mum 2: In South Africa when apartheid ended, all of a sudden it was okay for blacks and whites to marry. For a lot of people it must've been very hard to accept blacks and whites walking in the street together because they were brought up to think it wasn't normal. It's the same with this issue.

Mum 1: I think part of the shock for parents is that your children are having sexual urges, and I think whether they're gay or straight, that's a lot to cope with. That your child is now thinking like an adult.

6. 'Should we take our child to a doctor or psychiatrist?'

> *Rafe was making suicide attempts when he was at school. He did try to come out to the counsellor and she said to him, 'Don't even think about it, it's not an option.' The school talked about AIDS and negative things like that, but nothing positive about being GLBT.* **Gabby**

If you think your child needs to be 'cured', this is a fallacy. Same-sex attraction is not a disease or disorder. If your child is having trouble coming to terms with their sexual orientation, then it may help to get some counselling to foster their self-acceptance and self-esteem. Similarly, many child psychologists and medical practitioners are questioning the immediate application of the label 'gender identity disorder' (GID) to children, including intersexed children, who do not display or conform to social and/or physiological norms of masculinity and femininity. One way to assist children experiencing extreme gender dissatisfaction is to expand their options, letting them choose what they will be called, what they will wear, what activities they will participate in, and educating family members and schools about your child's needs and individuality. Under no circumstances should the child be blamed or pathologised for any harassment they receive because of their sexuality or gender.

> *I'm a school counsellor and I just hark back to what I was like five years ago, and what I'm like now, after my children have come out, which is like two different people. Many school counsellors do a lot of good things but some know very little really about GLBT people. I was forced into learning, and it worries me that school counsellors might have these homophobic attitudes without even realising that they have them. Training in GLBT issues isn't compulsory. I went along to one of the conferences after my daughter came out because I thought, 'I've got to learn something here.' It was excellent, but it was optional. Since then, I've been giving out brochures about courses to other counsellors.* **Gillian**

It was only recently that aversion therapy, electric shock treatments and medicines were used to 'cure' homosexuality. With time, these methods have been shown to be mistaken and damaging to the physical, emotional and mental health of the young person. Currently, medical, surgical and psychiatric intervention with intersexed babies or trans-gendered children is under question. Increasingly, parents are being advised to allow their children to grow with love and acceptance of who they are. Research with older intersexed and transgendered people is now documenting the damage that has been done to them as children via external interventions before they were of an age where they could make their own decisions about how they wish to express their gender, and to what extent they wish to undertake or feel they require 'gender reassignment' – hormonal, surgical or otherwise.

Ask yourself: what ways of being 'male' and 'female' are upheld as 'normal' in this society? How have these ways changed over time and place, from culture to culture? For example, 'cross-dressing' used to be applied to women in pants at the beginning of the twentieth century as well as men in dresses. Today, women in pants is 'normal', and 'cross-dressing' is something only some 'sick' men do. Is your child really unhappy with their gender or are they unhappy that they are made to feel like freaks if they don't conform to stereotyped sex-role embodiment, behaviour and dress?

If you as a parent are having difficulty accepting and affirming your child's sexuality or ways of doing masculinity/femininity, then it may be best to seek counselling and support for yourself. At no cost accept any counselling or medical intervention, or so-called 'support' of your child or yourself, that pathologises and makes a problem of your child's sexuality. Your child is fine. Your child would be very happy if it wasn't for a society and, yes, a social history of medical, psychological and psychiatric theories and interventions which have made homo-sexuality and gender diversity deviant, diseased, and something to be counselled about.

> *My daughter has a disability and when she came out at school I asked the counsellor about her being gay and he made the strange comment to me: 'Well it's only an act, because I know about disabilities, and disabled people are always straight.' Oh, I felt so sorry for him and for her and for all the others who are not getting their rights to express their sexuality. It's as if they're not going to have any sexuality if they're disabled and if they do, it is only heterosexual.* **A mum**

Counselling shouldn't be about the sexuality or the gender. It should focus on dealing with the social, mental and emotional problems others cause for your child and the family, and how to live one's life with resilience and self-confidence. When choosing a counsellor for your GLBT child, ask them questions such as the following:

▶▶ Have you had experience supporting and counselling GLBT young people?

▶▶ What kind of professional training have you had in regard to GLBT issues?

▶▶ What do you think about the idea that people can choose to be GLBT?

▶▶ Do you believe therapy can change my child's sexuality? Would you see that as part of your role?

▶▶ Do you think being GLBT is a problem we should be concerned about? What should be our concerns?

And take a look round their offices: do you see positive posters, literature and announcements regarding GLBT people? Listen to the language they use: is it gender inclusive and affirming of sexual diversity?

> After our son came out and we heard of all the difficulties he'd been through, like the bullying, we were really worried he'd attempt suicide. So we talked with a good counsellor on how we could support him as a family so he'd have us at least and hopefully not get to suicide. As parents we were scared we wouldn't be able to care for him the way we should. *A mum*

7. 'Will my child suffer discrimination?'

Unfortunately yes, but with increasing anti-homophobic awareness and activism, discrimination will decrease. As a parent, you can provide a buffer zone for your child against discrimination or cheer from the sidelines when they take on these issues themselves. Get to know your anti-discrimination laws; get to know which services are out there. Surround your children with love and support at home, and with a group of family, friends, community that can bolster them and affirm them from outside prejudice and ignorance. Provide lots of books, videos, outings and opportunities to chat. Challenge schools, community services, neighbours and friends if they discriminate against your children. Provide opportunities and information for your child on how to meet other GLBT youth in social and support groups, and find positive and inspirational GLBT adult mentors and role models.

> Like every other parent, I had big fears of gay bashing and of AIDS. I still have those fears. You still hear about people who go around 'poofter bashing' and I think, 'Why?' Things like that hurt if you hear it, and it is a reality and a big worry. *Rudy*

8. 'Why does our child have to flaunt their difference with their hairstyles, dress, voice, effeminate/butch behaviour?'

What's wrong or harmful about playing with clothing, make-up and hairstyles? Why do parents fuss over these things but readily give their kids toy guns, swords and soldiers' uniforms and all these violent computer games that just promote aggression? **Naomi**

In some cases, GLBT young people (like straight young people!) use clothing, hairstyles and make-up to rebel against or stand out in a social system that regulates and enforces conformity. In other cases, it's a test of your acceptance: for example, are they loved by their parents despite the pink and blue-striped Mohawk and 'I'm a butch dyke' tattoo? And in other cases, it's your child having a sense of freedom to be themselves – part of resisting the discrimination of being different is to relish being different. Usually for GLBT young people, there's a settling down period after the initial 'coming out'. If you can imagine being restrained for so long and then suddenly releasing yourself from those restraints, what must that immense feeling of freedom be like, and how would you fashion your body and your style in order to let the world know you will no longer allow it to repress you.

Ultimately, the world is made up of a lot of cultures and subcultures, including a lot of youth subcultures, each doing some 'flaunting' to differentiate and identify themselves. Why do people worry so much about so-called gay flaunting or lesbian flaunting, while 'flaunting' oneself as of a particular ethnicity, or as a rapper, surfie, punk, hippy causes less concern? Why worry about the 'gay lisp' or 'gay mannerism'? Do we worry about the way 'sportsjocks' talk, or the way ethnic minorities and other youth groups speak 'street-slang'? They are cultural ways of belonging and identifying with others like you, as well as a diversity of

ways that people have of speaking and moving their bodies that show they belong to certain subcultures and groups.

Look at how some ethnic minority girls speak and dress, how 'African-American hip-hoppers' speak and dress. So your gay son is wearing tight jeans and a glittery shirt? What's your straight son wearing to show he's part of a culture or performing a particular way of being a guy? Is he wearing baggy pants that precariously hang around his lower hips and scrape under his sneakered feet? Does he move his body or hold his body in certain ways? What about your straight daughter? How does she laugh or talk or do her hair and make-up to perform her gender and flaunt her sexuality in certain ways? How about those straight guys who keep their voices lowered so as to sound straight? Isn't that as much about trying to conform to a style or 'flaunt' a particular kind of masculinity?

As a parent, the issue again is consistency. What limits and boundaries do you negotiate with your heterosexual children and with your GLBT children about their clothing, hair, piercings, tattoos? What do you like or dislike about how your straight and GLBT children 'flaunt' their sexualities? Is there a difference? Why?

Also, how harmful is what the young person is doing? Does it matter what colour their hair or shirt is? Does it matter whether they take long strides or trip along in high heels? Enjoy the colour, the variety! Marvel at the creativity and expression of our young people.

Now for the nostalgia cringe question: what were you wearing and how were you speaking and walking and 'flaunting' when you were a teenager? Why did you do all that? Check out some photos of your younger days, how you fashioned and 'flaunted' your gender and sexuality. Just as you now might cringe at some of it while sighing with nostalgia at other bits of it, so too will your GLBT children do the same one day. (And for most of us, it doesn't always disappear with age! How are you still 'flaunting' your sexuality and gender, or doing a certain look to show you belong to a particular peer group?)

> When Mick had his sixteenth birthday, before he came out, his older brother was already out, so we decided to have a drag night. Everybody had to get dressed up in drag, and we all made a good effort. All the young people thought it was absolutely fantastic that here was Grandad, in his seventies, in a dress and a wig, having an absolute ball pretending to be a drag queen. Grandma got up there with him and they were singing an Abba song. These two beautiful young boys are bringing in a world that our family had not experienced because we're the type of people that basically just lived in our own backyard. *Debbie*

9. 'What about marriage and children? Now I won't get to be a grandparent.'

> *When I told my mother, the first thing she said was that she wasn't going to get any grandchildren, and I said, 'Well, you are, but not in the usual way.'* **Josh**

> *When people say my daughter won't be able to have children because of her sexuality, I turn around saying, 'She can biologically have children, it's not about her sexuality.'* **A mum**

Increasingly, societal attitudes and laws are changing to allow same-sex marriages and parenting. So you may get to be a grandparent and enjoy it as long as you acknowledge and celebrate that 'marriage' and 'family' are not the exclusive domains of heterosexual people, and that there are diverse ways of doing 'marriage' and 'family'.

> *I had a neighbour pop in last week, and something came up in conversation about homosexuals. 'Oh, they want to have children!' and he was shuddering and carrying on about the legal changes. 'They couldn't be good parents.' I've been a foster parent for fifteen years and I was very quick to tell him, 'I've had many, many children in my care that have been battered and bruised and abused by heterosexual couples.'* **Margaret**

Increasing legal recognition and social acceptance of same-sex marriages and families shouldn't be used to enforce a whole new set of expectations and regulations for GLBT young people. Some GLBT young people, like some straight young people, want to marry and have children. Other GLBT young people, like an increasing number of straight young people, will question the validity of marriage and may not want to have children.

Thus, while broadening the legal and cultural boundaries of 'marriage' and 'family' to include same-sex relationships is a necessary and fundamental social justice and human rights issue, it shouldn't be allowed to set up a new hierarchy where, for example, the 'good' and 'normal' gay guy or lesbian is the one who marries, is monogamous, and has a mortgage and kids; and the 'bad' or 'deviant' ones are those who remain single, childless and have several loving relationships.

As parents, we should be encouraging and supporting our GLBT and straight children to make decisions from a broad range of options for satisfying and loving interpersonal and familial relationships.

> Humour is very important. When I'm asked, 'Have you got any grandchildren?' I say, 'No, but I've got some grand cats,' so have a line ready. **A mum**

10. 'Is homosexuality a sin? Will my child go to hell?'

> *Parent 1:* It says in the Bible that man shall not lie down with another man.
>
> *Parent 2:* It also says thou shall not eat shell fish, that men can't get their hair trimmed, and that selling your daughter into slavery is okay.

The belief that homosexuality is a sin usually stems from Biblical references that have been and continue to be interpreted by some church leaders in ways that do not take account of the historical, sociocultural and political contexts of the time they were written, let alone the inaccurate scientific and anatomical knowledge about human procreation and sexuality. For many of the Old Testament tribes, having children was a priority for the survival and prosperity of the community. Right up to about 400 years ago, it was thought that the male 'seed' was a new human being itself while the mother's womb only provided an incubator. Therefore, any sexual activity that 'wasted the seed' meant the death of a valuable member of a tribe or church member. This included masturbation, homosexuality and coitus interruptus (withdrawal of the penis before ejaculation).

Think about other traditional religious beliefs that have been challenged and modified due to scientific thinking and exploration. Think about how shifts in religious thinking came only after centuries of struggle and the death or oppression of many. For example, although Aristotle and others had said that the earth was not flat, it took the church another 600 years before they conceded to this. Likewise, many scientists, social thinkers and those who dared to challenge church doctrine on a range of issues (such as Galileo, who dared to say the earth revolved around the sun), were imprisoned, exiled or burnt at the stake. Fundamentalist religious thinking about sexual diversity is experiencing the same challenges and eventually will have to concede that it was based on fallacious understandings, just like the 'flat earth Christians' eventually did.

> *There's not one religion that teaches hatred. Islam doesn't teach it, Buddhism doesn't. They don't preach hatred. It is man's interpretation.* **A mum**

As a parent, you will need to decide what aspects of your religious faith are important to you. Is it the focus on spiritual health, love, respect and the dignity of all human beings, including your GLBT children? Or is it the man-made regulations and dogma? It may be difficult for you to hold on to everything you've believed to date, and still have a positive, loving relationship with your child. You don't have to abandon all your religious beliefs. Indeed, abandoning all the beliefs that mean so much to you may lead you to resent your child and feel that you've lost the anchor or meaning in your own life. On the other hand, sticking rigidly to your religious beliefs may impair your ability to be an anchor for your GLBT children. It may drive your child away and lead them to engage in self-destructive and suicidal behaviour if they also believe in those religious rules. And is that what your religious faith would want your child to do? Where's the love of family and supportive parenting that religious beliefs teach us?

So, find a way to hold on to the parts of your religion that sustain and encourage you to be a loving parent to your children. Think about the central messages of your religion, not the rules. Let your parenting reflect the central meanings of love, support and respect of your child. Let your religious beliefs and values work for you, not against you and your child. Ultimately, you will need to decide: What is more important to me, the religious beliefs I hold, or the health and wellbeing of my child?

> *I'm a mother of three sons and my youngest son is my gay son. In our family we're strong Catholics and one of the reasons he didn't come out is because I was a strong Catholic, so he had that barrier to cross. You have to reassure them that no matter where they go or what they do, gay or not, that you trust and love them, and they can come home with anything.* **Bernadette**

Some day homosexuality will be taken for granted and the question that will be asked by future religious leaders and their followers will be: 'Why did it take so long to understand and acknowledge the diversity of human sexuality? What was all the fuss about? Homophobia is sinful, not homosexuality.'

It all depends on if you want the church to change its mind, and I do, and so I'm prepared to fight for my children and their rights in the church because they have the same values as I have. They believe in God, and they live their lives in that respect. Not all the church is against homosexuality. You get pockets of the church that are there to support. If we all sit back and never try to make the church change its attitude, then it won't. You have to challenge the church. **A mum**

'You were created,' that's what I told my son. 'It's between you and God. If you feel your conscience is clear, you go to church, you go to communion. It's got nothing to do with the priest.' **Mary**

Be clued in from the start
YGLAM Youth Group

– I think parents need to be clued in from the start. I think nearly every parent makes the assumption that their kid's going to grow up to be heterosexual, and when they see signs otherwise, I think they tend to deny it.

– I know of a few parents that actually ask their kid before they're ready or before they've got themselves confident about it. I think it's more about parents just showing, demonstrating, that they're okay with it, and at least you get the idea that, 'Okay, my parents should be able to deal reasonably with this.'

– I think the problem is that a lot of parents don't actually realise they're homophobic until the child has come out. So, they have a certain politics or religious belief, like that's their view and perception unless it's challenged.

– I don't understand why every parent can't do and say positive things about being gay when their child's growing up, whether they think their child's going to be gay or not. They're just constantly geared for this one hetero way of living life.

Many parents say they 'always knew' their child was 'different' but didn't say or do anything. Many later query whether they should've 'come out that we knew, before the kids came out' in order to make it easier for their GLBT children. Research has found that GLBT children who are raised in families where the anti-homophobic groundwork has been done do have an easier time of it. Indeed, all families should be doing this groundwork and setting the scene for the possibility of having GLBT family members from the moment children are born, or in order to ensure that their straight children are raised as affirming and accepting of sexual and gender diversity, thus leading the way in creating further social change in schools, workplaces and local communities. A GLBT child coming out usually has not gone through a period of what Robert Merton in 1957 called 'anticipatory socialisation'. In other words, parents, families and the wider communities and culture don't prepare children to be GLBT. Children may lack an affirming vocabulary with which to talk about GLBT issues. They may also not have the opportunity of seeing lots of different ways of being GLBT, to grow up with GLBT people, information and same-sex feelings as part and parcel of everyday life.

You don't have to put the young person on the spot or push them to come out before they're ready. Create safe space in your family that would make them feel comfortable coming out. Create an environment that is receptive to diversity, dialogue and debate. It's difficult to teach our children to respect social diversity. We need to live it. They need to see us talking about and interacting with a variety of people and respecting their differences – modelling speaks louder than words. Let them hear you talking about GLBT news items and daily incidents in a way that expresses where you stand. If you have GLBT friends, invite them to events where your children are present.

Many GLBT young people say they often 'test' their parents to see where they stand on GLBT issues. There are so many opportunities to voice your views without directly involving your children. If you're watching a TV show and there's something discriminatory or intimidating or threatening to a gay character, say, 'I don't like to think that things like that happen to gay people and I would never let that happen in my family. I hope it doesn't happen in our neighbourhood or your schools.' Let your children hear you challenge the homophobia of radio DJs as you drive along in your car. They may think you're a bit looney talking back to a radio or TV or newspaper, but the message about where you stand on these issues comes through loud and clear. It's giving them a green light to go ahead and come out to you.

Make what I call WWW statements about sexuality and sexual expression: 'Whenever you have sex, Whoever you have sex with, and Whatever you do, make sure it's emotionally, physically and sexually safe and satisfying for yourself and the other person.' Or begin sentences with inclusive phrases: 'When you start dating a guy or girl or both … '

> *I'd always been told when I was young that being gay is okay, and that if I ever had a boyfriend, to make sure to bring him around.* **Neth**

Not every parent goes through feelings of denial, anger, depression and grief when their children come out. An increasing number of parents are supportive and affirming from the beginning. The following parents, Joanne and Michael, have a lesbian daughter, Jasmin, who is a highly acclaimed and much loved youth worker. They say that it's actually just part of parenting to love and support your children and be prepared and affirming of whatever their sexuality is going to be. But they also show that it may not be that simple for the child. Providing an affirming environment, even with mum and dad having GLBT friends, doesn't always convince children that you'll accept them, your own kids.

Joanne and Michael also challenge the assumption that there seems to be an age when you can begin to talk to your children about these issues. They believe these issues should just be part of everyday conversations in the home as children are growing up.

I hated the way I was asking questions to Joanne and Michael about what made them so open and accepting, as if they were the freaks because they didn't follow the stages of denial, grief and acceptance as put down by some manual.

We never saw it as a problem
Joanne and Michael

Joanne: I grew up in a very strict Presbyterian family, and I know my father was very, very straight about everything. But I can't remember ever realising that gay people were supposedly different to anyone else. I had a cousin who was gay, and that was fine by me. I can't even remember how I found out, but it was never discussed in our family, certainly not with my parents. When AIDS came out, my stepmother said to me after my father had died, 'Your father always knew this would happen – it's a punishment. Leviticus, he always said. Read Leviticus.' And I thought, 'No way am I going to read Leviticus.'

So when Jasmin came out, it wasn't a problem for me. I remember Jasmin wrote an article in her university magazine about how her coming out to us sort of lacked drama. She was quite disappointed because nothing happened. We just said, 'Well, we know,' and I can't even imagine why she would've ever thought there would've been a drama. Probably because so many other kids had a drama she thought she might just get a little one, but she didn't.

Michael: I think my upbringing was a little bit different to Joanne's. I think my family was a bit more easygoing about those sort of things, but, nonetheless, a lot of jokes were made about homosexuals and I can remember when I was about fifteen, my mother had a godson who was gay and he got up her nose a bit about something and there was a bit of a kerfuffle in the family. My father and my brother said, 'Well if anybody in our family was gay like that, we'd boot them out straight away. We wouldn't want them living in our house.' So I learnt early on that this was something that you could not possibly be, it's not acceptable.

A couple of years later, I had a best friend at school who told us he was gay when he was about seventeen. He killed himself. In our era people didn't talk about being gay in an intelligent way. I told my parents about him and I was not allowed to see him again. Being a child of an establishment family who didn't want anything like that and was terrified of anything like that, I did the wrong thing and stopped seeing him, and I've regretted that ever since. His family did dreadful things. His parents put him into a mental hospital, and eventually he killed himself. I think that was branded on my mind. That was a very big life lesson to learn when you're around seventeen. I've had to carry it around. So that was the background I came into parenting with. I think I've got a very big investment in not ever seeing anything like this happen to anyone else. It's important to give parents the message that you have to be very careful to not damage this child of yours.

Joanne: One thing I probably should add is that our best friend, Alan, who's about twenty years younger than us, is gay and he used to spend heaps and heaps of time at home with us. The family over the road from us had two little boys that used to play with our girls. The boys used to dress up as girls and they used to all have lovely times with handbags and dress-ups. One day, their mother came over and said to us, 'Peter, my husband, doesn't want the boys to dress up any more with your girls.' And I said, 'Well, why on earth not?'

'Because they might turn out to be gay.'

I said, 'Well, Sue, I can't see how that's got anything to do with it.'

'Well, if you had boys you wouldn't have Alan as your best friend.'

'Yes, we would.'

I think Jasmin might've been about sixteen and one of her sisters and I decided that definitely she could be gay because she used to look at boys and sort of say, 'Mm, mm, look at him, isn't he terrific,' but there was no twinkle in her eye whatsoever. I know she went to some counselling at the university about why she couldn't keep relationships and I just kept on thinking, 'Well, when is she going to find out?' But we actually didn't think we had the right to tell her what we thought because it was up to her to find out. If we said 'Okay, I'm quite sure you're gay', then that might interrupt her thinking about it. But later on, she said to us, 'Well, why didn't you tell me?' and I said, 'Well, you really had to find out yourself.' She said, 'It would've made it so much easier.'

Michael: Jasmin put up quite a good performance. She went out with boys, but they weren't successful relationships. I didn't really think about her being straight or gay particularly. It wasn't something I actually gave much thought to and when it came up, I certainly wasn't surprised, which is quite interesting. I didn't have a reaction like, 'Oh, God, I didn't know that she was.' I just thought, 'Well, I must've been a bit dumb, I didn't pick up on some of the signs that were being put out.'

Joanne: We were in London and Jasmin wrote to us, 'Guess what, I'm gay' in huge, great big letters and I said, 'Well, okay, I know,' and we didn't do anything instantly. She rang us up and said, 'Did you get my letter?'

We said, 'Yes.'

'Well?'

I said, 'Well, I thought you probably were anyway. So that's okay, you're gay.'

Michael: It seemed like a bit of a non-event and I'm sort of surprised that I didn't react a little bit more, but I didn't. Beth, our other daughter, was quite boyish and she used to like dressing up as a boy when she was little and drawing on a moustache. She actually talked to me once when she was younger, asking me, 'What would you do if I was gay and liked other girls?' I said, 'If that's how you feel and that feels right to you then it's absolutely fine with me.' I think if I'd been a bit more cluey in as much as Jasmin went through a lot of anxiety and anguish trying to be straight and if she'd been like Beth when she was thirteen and said, 'Do you think I could be gay?' then you can open it up and you can actually say things which can help a lot, because Jasmin did go through agonies with some of those boys that she tried to be so-called 'normal' with.

Joanne: And being the parents we were, I thought that if she felt like that, she'd tell us anyway. I never dreamt that it was up to us to tell her and she really wished we had.

Michael: We had already gone through parent effectiveness training quite early on when our eldest daughter was fifteen. I'd had tremendous rows with her. I was very nervous about the way she didn't quite conform at school so we did parent effectiveness training and that made us far more open to listening. Joanne never had much of a problem listening. But I think I did have that problem. You do the best you can at the time, but, yes, it is important to have that open environment where they can talk about these things.

Joanne: Yes. We bought books about raising teenagers like I imagine many parents do, about growing up and becoming a boy and girl and all that sort of thing but it was always that eventually the boy and the girl get a boyfriend and a girlfriend. But they knew that Alan was gay and that was fine. I don't think we ever actually stated, 'Maybe when you get older, it might be that one of you might like a girl.' But even if she'd come to me at five, I would've been supportive because it's never been an issue with me.

Michael: At work, people say, 'Have you got grandchildren? Are your children married?' and I just say, 'Yes, I have one daughter who's married, one who's married and has a baby, and I have another who is gay who is in a relationship. She's in a partnership and had a civil celebrant marrying them.' I definitely make a big point, if the opportunity comes up and they ask about my children, to talk about each one equally.

Joanne: We haven't got the type of friends that'd say, 'Oh God, how awful.' Whenever I get an opportunity I tell people that I'm the mother of Jasmin, who is gay, and I've never had anyone at work say anything about it. I can't remember anyone actually looking particularly perturbed about it. Maybe it's because I'm so accepting. It's interesting, once you're accepting and loving, you suddenly find other young people who don't get that with their own parents seeing you as a mentor, an adult who's there to actually say you're okay.

Michael: A lot of the kids in Jasmin's youth groups, when we talk to them, they say, 'Oh, you're Jas's parents. Gosh, we wish we had parents like you.'

Joanne: And at Jasmin and Vonnie's wedding, oh, everybody was just so excited. It was wonderful and they said, 'Oh, if only my parents could see this, if only my parents could see this and be accepting and supportive like you.'

Michael: Wouldn't it be wonderful if we didn't actually have to talk about it, being straight or being gay? I'm sure some people could be really loving, supportive parents, but unless they're prepared to accept that child on an equal basis with their heterosexual child, no amount of loving or anything will get them through that. I find it so hard to believe that the parent could have the child one minute that they love and adore and have a perfect, happy relationship, and because the child says, 'Well, actually I'm gay,' they suddenly don't love that child any more. That child is exactly the same child they were two minutes ago. So, yes, we provided a really good background for Jasmin, lots of love and backing, and we also understood about our kids being able to be different.

Another thing to say to parents: if you think your child is gay and you feel that you are able to talk to them about it, talk about it because they'll either say they are or they'll say, 'I'm not, don't talk to me about it,' and then you can say, 'Well if it happens, it's fine with us.' A lot of parents don't talk about it. They have suspected their child has been gay but they don't want to talk about it and the child probably knows they're gay and they're probably all sitting around really wishing they could do something but they don't do it.

Hanging out the 'dirty washing?': parents coming out about their children's coming out

Susan: If questions come up like, 'Oh, has Christopher got a girlfriend yet?' I'll usually say, 'No, but he's got a boyfriend.' I just say it really, really casually, and then they go, 'Oh, right.' They don't know that I'm absolutely shaking in my boots. As brave as we all are, I shit myself basically. Excuse what I've said, but that's how I feel. It's very, very hard, with some family and friends and people you meet, but you do it. My attitude is that you have to face things. It's the only way I can get on in life. I just have to tell people upfront.

I told one girlfriend and she said, 'Oh, I feel so privileged that you've taken me into your confidence.' I wasn't quite sure how to take that. I said, 'Well, would you have said that if I'd said Christopher had a girlfriend?' 'No.' Even though it was kind of nice, because she was accepting him, it was still like, 'Oh, you poor thing. But thank you for telling me.' I thought, 'No, I don't want it to be that I'm just telling you in confidence as if it's a secret to be hidden. I want to tell you that it's just normal, an everyday sort of thing.' And that's basically how I come out and say it.

I've had another person say to me, 'Wow, you said that really well. Gee, you said it so confidently.' And I'm thinking, 'Well yeah, because it's just telling you. You asked me a question and I said yes, he's got a boyfriend.' I think when people see that you're comfortable, you're confident, it's just normal, it's natural, they might feel the same way. Whether or not they really understand, I don't know, but then again, it's a start. Just take that stand and do it.

Kathy: I've taken videos, newspaper stories and books with GLBT themes to work and given them to other people. I'm not the type of person that gets up there and waves a flag all the time, but because it touches my life on a daily basis, I'm sharing it with people and it's opening their eyes up more.

At some point, you'll begin to tell your relatives and friends that your child is GLBT. And you'll know or get the feeling that some of them will respond in negative ways. Be clear about your motives for making the disclosure. Is it something you've discussed with your child; is it what they want, and will it be beneficial for them? Or has your coming out got something to do with a personal grievance, anger or other conflict issue between you and your relatives and friends? Your child's sexuality shouldn't be used as a weapon with which you fight your own battles.

Choose a time and place to talk when you won't be interrupted. Make sure you're feeling emotionally strong. Then let them know calmly and confidently.

My mother and father were people that we didn't feel we could discuss the issue with, but my mother actually came to me and said, 'I believe one of your boys is gay.'
I said, 'Well, yes, actually three of them are.'
And she was wonderful right from the start.
We hadn't felt we could go to them because they were an older generation and wouldn't understand. We still didn't tell my dad straight away, but when we did, he said that he couldn't believe that we would think he wouldn't love them.
My children are travelling a lot at the moment. Mum, particularly, writes letters to them regularly, phones them regularly, and they now do the same with her. They're much closer to her and Dad than they ever were. **Brenda**

I think if you walk positively with your children, wherever you are – in a restaurant, in a party – if you walk around feeling proud of yourself and your family, it flows through a little bit. **Sue**

Most GLBT young people will want their parents to tell at least some of their relatives and friends. If that's the case and you refuse to, it can be quite devastating for a child to hear that you're more worried about what your own parents or relatives or friends will think about you than how your child feels. You're old enough to no longer need your parents' and relatives' approval. You're also old enough to be very selective about your friendships and not need the absolute approval of your peers. Your child needs to see you being the strong and secure adult who deals resiliently with conflict and prejudice so that they can also grow up that way.

When I first found out, I didn't know how friends, family, work colleagues, anybody was going to accept it. I suppose initially I felt ashamed. Anybody that knows me now knows I'm very proud of my son. Anybody that scorns me or my son would no longer be a friend. **Elaine**

After our son Neil came out, his dad, Keith, came out to his mother. This was against my better judgement, but it turned out to be fine. She's terrific with Neil because she really loves him and they get on well together. From time to time if we're not around, they might have lunch together or something like that. When she met Neil's first boyfriend at Neil's twenty-first birthday party, she said, 'Isn't he a spunk!' and he was. I was amazed to think that she was offering that comment.

The only thing she wanted was that her grandson being gay was to be kept private. She didn't want any publicity about her grandson or our family. But Neil and I agreed to do an article for a women's magazine and Keith's mother was ready to move to the moon. As a family, we were really thrilled to have the opportunity to help other families through doing this magazine article. She was the only dissenting voice and I said to her at the time, 'I'm sorry you don't agree with what we're doing but it's too important not to do it. I respect what you're thinking, but I've got to act the way I feel.'

The magazine showed some family photographs so we were easily identifiable. Keith's mother said, 'All my friends will buy it and read it, and they'll see the family photos!' She was really distressed. As it turned out, she got only one comment.

As you know, these magazines survive on and on in dentists' and doctors' waiting rooms. Some months later, a colleague of Keith's phoned him and said, 'I'd been waiting in the dentist's room and reading this magazine and I found your article.' Keith was very taken aback as he didn't know what this man's reaction would be, but the colleague was very supportive and said, 'I think your family's very brave for doing it.' **Narelle**

All the family know and all our friends know, so Jay is completely at ease with everyone. I think that's made a big difference. But it took a while to get to that point. Probably my dad was the one that we were worried about telling most of all as he's from the old school. When I told him Jay was gay, he was very shocked, but he said that it didn't make any difference to him, and that he would always love the two boys the same. So, that was a really special thing for us.

Dad belongs to the bowling club and all the old boys down there are fairly homophobic. One day, there was a gay joke, and my dad actually said that he really didn't like where that was going, that he had a grandson who was gay. I think they just couldn't believe it.

Our son also does drag and Dad's been fantastic with that. He hasn't come to see a show, but the two grandmothers have, and they just think he's wonderful. **Jan**

I think families can surprise you. I've got a 92-year-old aunt who died this week and she had a photo of my partner and me on her dressing table in the nursing home. She was just fantastic. **A niece**

I come from a South American background, and my parents have a lot of extended family and friends. I remember them telling me when I came out, 'We don't want our friends and families to know,' and I kind of agreed, 'Yeah, it's your right.' So I left it in their hands. It's been six years now since they've known. I had my graduation last year and I said, 'I want to invite my friends and the family.' They said 'Sure' and actually told everyone else in our extended family: 'We're having Ed's graduation. By the way, you know, he's gay. I hope you don't have a problem.' So, I think it's about giving them time. **Ed**

Our daughter's coming out was made easier because our family is based on real traditional values. If the family's very well endowed with love, you'll handle so many things together. We came through as a family. My daughter decided that she'd make an announcement in a general conversation with the whole family present. She made it quite clear that she was a lesbian and that was her sexuality, which should be no problem for anybody else, and I had to say that my family came on board very well. I think we can teach people in our families to be accepting and open-minded. **A mum**

I've been on educational videos, on radio, television, and in newspapers, and my family don't speak to me about it. I think there's denial and I also think that sometimes because it's alien to their family and their reality, they don't quite know what to say to you. They should realise they can just say exactly the same things we say and ask about their children. **A dad**

Telling a GLBT child's younger siblings may require extra sensitivity. They may be anxious about their own status at school or worried about the reactions of their own peers. Sometimes they may resent the extra attention the older sibling is getting, or resent the disruption to the family or their own lives in the community.

I have a thirteen-year-old son who goes to a Catholic school and he's very proud of Matthew. At his school he has a few homophobic teachers, and he said to me 'Oh, Mum, I used to like Mr – but I don't any more because he's passed comment about gays.' He has asked me, 'Mum, is it all right for me to tell my friends at school that Matthew's gay?' And I said, 'Well, of course, yes.' **Elaine**

'But he's coloured!'

James Adcock

Coming out to my grandparents was something I particularly dreaded. I was close to them, and they were always proud of me. Would anything change once they learnt about my sexuality? They seemed to be so old and so narrow-minded. I decided not to tell them.

However, I hadn't counted on my grandmother's sister, who lived around the corner from me. One day she saw my boyfriend, Paul, and me in the supermarket. She put two and two together, and immediately came up and introduced herself to him.

My dear great-aunt could not keep her secret for long. The news spread quickly throughout my large extended family. My cousins thought it most exciting that I was gay! I was asked if I would like to bring my boyfriend along to the next family function – my cousin's fancy-dress twenty-first birthday party. 'We're dying to meet him!' they said.

As my grandparents would be there, I was concerned about bringing him. But I was assured that as there'd be so many people there, he could easily blend in. So I agreed to bring him.

On the night, I was dressed in a devil suit, and Paul was dressed as a Native American Indian. While Paul was delighted to meet my extended family, he also said he didn't feel he belonged. He was the only one of the hundred guests who was not white. I hadn't noticed.

Not long into the night, my grandfather sidled up asking me to point out Paul. I almost choked on my carrot stick. *Did he know Paul was my boyfriend*? Hesitantly, I pointed out the Indian, who was taking over the dance floor. 'But he's coloured!' my grandfather exclaimed. I'd only expected him to be homophobic, not racist!

I still don't know exactly what my great-aunt said to my grandparents, but whatever it was, they're still as proud of me as ever, and always ask about Paul. I think that's pretty good.

For my sister with love
Aunty Lois

You have a Son,
That you know is Gay,
Give him your love,
Don't turn him away.

God gave him these feelings
That come from within.
We don't understand them,
We couldn't even begin.

The choice was not his,
How could it be.
He knew he was different,
From the age of three.

Can you imagine the hurt
He suffered alone.
Afraid of being ridiculed,
Through no fault of his own.

He needs your love and support,
Even more than most,
He's your Son,
Stand up and boast.

You have other children,
But don't push him aside.
Let him stand tall in the family,
And hold his head up with pride!

When you get asked dumb questions about your children ... ask smart questions right back!

Question the questions.

Question why the questions are asked in the first place.

Question what it is about our societies and communities that makes the questions seem valid and 'normal'.

▶▶ 'What caused your child's homosexuality?'

What caused your heterosexuality? What caused your children's heterosexuality?

▶▶ 'When did your child decide to be homosexual?'

When did you decide to be heterosexual? Do you recall your children deciding to be heterosexual?

▶▶ 'Is it possible this is just a phase they'll grow out of?'

Have you/will you/why don't you grow out of your heterosexual phase? Does this mean your children might grow out of their heterosexual phase?

▶▶ 'If they've never had sex with an opposite sex person, how do they know?'

Did you have sex with a same-sex person before you knew you were straight? Did you know before you were having any sex at all?

▶▶ 'Why does your child flaunt their homosexuality?'

What does that mean? Does that mean opposite-sex couples in advertisements, birth-day cards, magazines, those touching, hugging and kissing in restaurants and on the streets, are flaunting their heterosexuality? Does that mean you and your children are flaunting your heterosexuality? Could you keep your heterosexuality quiet? Would you want to? Would you want your children to?

▶▶ 'Why do homosexuals place too much emphasis on sex?'

Have you looked around your straight culture lately? Billboards, car adverts, food adverts, MTV, magazines, movies, novels, the Internet? How much sex are your children seeing, hearing, and experiencing in their everyday lives?

▶▶ **'Why do homosexuals recruit people into their lifestyle?'**

So all this heterosexual culture around us isn't recruiting people into being straight, getting married, etc etc? Some GLBT people get recruited into that straight world and then have to re-find themselves later. Are your sexual desires a lifestyle?

▶▶ **'Why are homosexuals paedophiles?'**

Why are 80 percent of child molesters heterosexual men, usually known to children as family members? And why are the majority of children that get molested little girls, molested by straight men?

▶▶ **'Just what do they do in bed if they can't have sexual intercourse?'**

Is that all you do? There's lots of ways of being sexual, and there are sexual practices that can be done by both opposite-sex and same-sex couples. If you're wondering about anal sex, just like some straights don't do vaginal sex, some straights do anal sex, and some GLBTs don't.

▶▶ **'Why are there so few stable lasting relationships among homosexuals?'**

Why is the divorce rate for straights so high, despite the huge amount of social approval and legal support? Why are there a lot of extra-marital affairs? Why are so many people unhappy even if they stay married?

OF COURSE IF YOU WERE **MARRIED** TO STEVE YOU'D BE QUITE WELCOME TO BRING HIM... BUT THAT'S NOT GOING TO HAPPEN...

KENTON PENLEY

'The world did not stop spinning': a Christian mother remembers

Jan Coleman

The world did not stop spinning and there was no crash of thunder but it was quite a shock all the same.

A few years ago she told the two of us, her parents, while we were still sitting around the table after dinner. Her youngest sibling had just gone back upstairs to study, that old familiar excuse for getting out of the washing up. We were about to get coffee.

'There's something I want to tell you both,' she said. Split-second thoughts started to form but she continued immediately. 'I'm a lesbian,' she said, and burst into tears.

Thank God for her openness and love. Thank God also for hugs and closeness. We all sprang up from the table and held each other for quite some time, voices muffled in shoulders and jumpers. Her frame felt thin and vulnerable through her weeping, but then a bit of laughter began creeping in, and at last we all settled back down and began to talk about the new dimension in our lives.

Being a parent is such a privilege. Brings with it myriad joys and delights, and a fair degree of confusion and angst. That night there was deep gratitude that our daughter had told us about another of her realities but also an ineffable sadness. I envisioned her vital young life as henceforth being filled with restrictions. There would be so many difficulties in her path that I had never had to face.

As it has turned out, it has been a very interesting couple of years' growth for us. For a long time after that night, I probably found myself listening more carefully to her when she talked about her feelings and I would bring up lesbian issues to see if she wanted to discuss anything. Must have been a bit dreary, really, looking back.

But for almost a year I found it very difficult to talk to anybody outside the immediate family about her homosexuality. It was quite often pointed out by my brutally truthful progeny that this was my own problem and that they and their generation had no such difficulties. I kept thinking of so many of my acquaintances who derided or dismissed gays and lesbians as queer (of course!), laughable or dangerous. Their imagined reaction scared me off. I had no courage. Caitlin suggested sometimes that I tell a few close friends 'in your own good time'. I demurred. 'It might not be easy being green,' I would say lamely, 'and it's so much easier being yellow.'

I began talking about it with a few friends. I chose these carefully either because of their understanding natures or because certain things were happening in their own families that had made them more sensitive to others.

Inch by inch. One day Caitlin brought home yet another pamphlet about a discussion group for people interested in the rights and dignity of homosexuals within the church. That was another stepping stone in my loosening up process. At this gathering I met and got to know a group of people, mainly GLBT and Christian, who voiced their yearning to be full participating members of their church and the pain they had encountered.

Through that meeting, I have had the opportunity to become a little involved with several Christian support groups for GLBT people and others who are marginalised. There are all kinds of religious groups in our midst – just a phone call or Internet click away. There are meetings, demonstrations, and reflection days at which GLBT and their friends and supporters can express their struggles and disillusionment, the empowering and enrichment they find in different facets of their lives. I keep going to some of these because I feel strongly for what they are trying to achieve – and I come away feeling enriched also.

Caitlin and I laugh when we reflect how – even though it was she who alerted me to most of these groups in the first place, and went to one or two of them herself – she then decided they weren't for her. She's involved in a couple of meaningful support groups in the Baptist and Uniting Churches and has a good group of friends within those communities. She has a fulfilling job in a difficult area of social work and is a most outstanding young woman living strong Christian values.

So, here is an age-old issue that has now entered our lives in a very personal way. There are other issues, too, within the church and society that need to be explored on this faith journey. I feel that Christ is lovingly in the midst of those who feel alienated and that He affirms and graces, offering hope and healing.

For me, some of these growth gifts, like the Eucharist, my weekly prayer and discussion group, personal prayer, and prayer with those closest to me, have now taken on a more meaningful perspective.

At last year's Gay Festival I decided to march with the GLBT

Christian groups and asked Caitlin whether she'd be marching too, as she had the previous year under another banner. She explained that she'd arranged to watch it from the sidelines this time with a group of friends. But they reconsidered and marched with us, 'to show our support for you supporting us!'

After the march, Caitlin's group went to join the huge crowd sitting on the beach listening to the bands belting out the decibels. I went back home to my other reality, a comfy, easy late afternoon with others in the family, going for a walk, watching the brilliant sunset over the city skyline, having something simple for dinner.

Good things, relationships.

'You suddenly have more children':

Mothers talk about supporting their children's partners

— My son's partner is Singaporean. He misses his mum in Singapore and I'm his mum here.

— My daughter Sue came out two years ago when she was nearly seventeen. She's got support because our family has a long tradition of having gay women in it. But my daughter's first girlfriend, her parents went slightly ballistic, threatening to throw her out of the house while she still had her final year of high school to complete. She was an only child from a very strict Catholic family and they had given her everything: phone, car, the whole lot. The phone got taken off, the car got taken off, and her life became a nightmare. Meanwhile, she's coming out, in love with my daughter, and trying to successfully complete high school. I was saying to Sue, 'If things get really bad, she can stay at our place.'

One evening, I was summoned to their house to talk to her parents. I admit I lied through my teeth because I'd known for some time about our girls who now wanted me to pretend I knew nothing about what was going on. This girl had her final school formal coming up, with my daughter going as her partner. And they begged me not to say anything. They had primed me before, 'Don't say this, don't say that.' So, I went down and talked to the mother who asked, 'But the whole thing she's going through, it's just a stage, isn't it?'

Now what was I going to say? I'm trying to support this poor girl and my daughter so I did the whole thing: 'Oh, maybe it is a phase.' Lie, lie, lie. That evening was a bit of a nightmare. I don't like lying but I lied through my teeth so that Sue's girlfriend didn't cop it at such an important time of her life. I wanted to deflect some of their anger and frustration from this poor girl who had enough troubles without her parents totally overreacting and chucking spasms. As parents we have to make a decision to support our children and that means supporting their partners. Just by saying that I accepted what was going on, now and again joking with her about stuff, just being there if she needed an adult to speak to, made a big difference for Sue's partner. I could see that she was a total mess. And yes, my daughter's name became mud around the parent circles. But we stood by them.

— My daughter's really happy. She's in a relationship, but her girl-friend's parents don't accept it, don't even acknowledge it. I've got to try my best to support her because she says she gets jealous of my daughter's and my relationship and that causes a bit of conflict between my daughter and her. She's just been accepted into a uni-versity in another city so her parents are really happy. They think they can buy an apartment for her up there and get her away from my daughter. It's really hard to handle all this sometimes. We've just got through hard times with my daughter, it was all very trau-matic getting our family and friends to support her. Now they do, we have a lot of support as a family. And it's great to see her really happy, but it's like we have to go through more with her partners. But I think that's the thing as a parent, you just keep accepting and supporting them.

Part 2:

When our children come out in schools

For many GLBT young people, the school years are some of the most difficult times of their lives as well as the most detrimental to their health and wellbeing. Adolescence can be particularly tough to get through as it's a time when 'fitting in', 'being cool', exploring one's sexuality, performing a 'normal' masculinity and femininity, and figuring out one's future place in the world are challenging enough – without realising that you're expected to do all that, but only as a heterosexual.

There is so much that can be done to make a GLBT young person's schooldays a time of fulfilling and empowering exploration and education about the self and the world. It's so obvious and should be so simple that even eight-year-old Abe Whyte, in the following, is able to identify homophobia in schools and what can be done. If only some adults could perceive what education should really be about with the clarity of young people like Abe!

If I were a teacher
Abe Whyte (eight years old)

If I were a teacher, I would try to teach kids about homosexuality, lesbianism, and things about homophobia etc.

I would teach them that being homophobic is like being racist – hating someone because they are different.

I would teach them that just like people have different religious choices they can have different sexual choices too.

I've asked many kids why they think being gay is bad, and they say, 'Because it's sick.' So I ask, 'Why is it sick?' And they reply 'Because … because … it's different'. 'So why is different bad?' Most people by now would have either walked away or just stood there thinking, until saying, 'It just is!'

If I were a teacher, I would get kids to express their thoughts and feelings about the topic. I would show them that even though being lesbian or gay may seem weird to them, it doesn't mean they're mentally unstable, and sexuality is only one part of a person.

Most kids I know would discriminate against everything about someone, just because they're gay!

And as a teacher, I wouldn't let anyone in my class be picked on because their parent was lesbian or gay. I wouldn't let a kid get bashed either because of their parent.

I would show kids that lesbians and gays aren't different, they are loving, funny, friendly and natural just like most other people.

In many schools, students are taking control themselves. They're forming little support groups and they're talking to their school counsellor and their principal. I went along to a school forum and there were three wonderful young people who just spoke so beautifully. They were so positive about things that they were doing in their school to end homophobia. They were so pro-active, setting up strategies. Quite inspirational listening to them. **A mum**

Cleaning out by coming out!

As parents, families and teachers in our communities, we have major roles to play in encouraging, supporting, and indeed insisting, that our schools respond to homophobia as they do to other prejudices, such as sexism and racism, within the broader educational frameworks of social justice and student welfare.

Schools need to take action to clean out the homophobia that's affecting the health and education of our young people. It may take a lot of scrubbing, some gentle soaking, and some strategic pegging on the clothesline: not too much sun at first, enough shade and shelter so that the initial efforts don't get buffeted by storms and bird droppings. But put on the washing gloves, make it a team effort, and clean OUT your school.

Twenty implementation ideas for the three Ps: Policies, Pastoral practices and Pedagogy

1. Develop policies that name homophobic harassment and heteronormative discrimination.

2. Collect data about parent, staff and student attitudes; levels of harassment; what's included in or excluded from the curriculum.

3. Offer support groups and social clubs for GLBT students.

4. Offer work experience opportunities to students at GLBT organisations.

5. Provide counselling and support for whole families: siblings, parents, etc.

6. Create a culture of affirmation and celebration via assemblies, guest speakers, posters, book displays, and acknowledgement of significant historical and current events.

7. Discuss fears and ignorance rather than condoning them through curriculum and pedagogical silence.

8. Build on the core values of the school: school motto, school billboard, school mission statement.

9. Teach and use the laws and policies of your state.

10. When conducting employment interviews with potential teachers, counsellors and other staff, include questions and discussion about their professional experiences in and personal attitudes to working with GLBT young people and their families.

11. Include anti-homophobia in any information night held with parents as part and parcel of the duty of care of the school.

12. Set up links with community services and persons dealing with GLBT issues, collect teaching resources and packages and material for the library.

13. Review and revise any activities that specify opposite-sex issues and discriminate against same-sex attracted students and their families, e.g. school dances, family activities.

14. Review school textbooks and other curriculum materials and contact local bookshops and GLBT centres for supplementary materials.

15. Organise professional development of teachers that includes sessions on anti-homophobia.

16. Develop prejudice awareness among student leaders and make an anti-homophobic school culture that affirms and celebrates sexual diversity one of their initiatives.

17. Provide opportunities for GLBT studies, research and assignments.

18. Encourage all students to think about, voice and write about how homophobia has impacted on their lives. Teachers can lead these discussions with talks about their own lives.

19. Display GLBT materials alongside other materials on noticeboards and in other public places in the school.

20. Make anti-homophobia part of the everyday public culture in assemblies, newsletters, etc., along with discussions and presentations of other issues. For example, hold a social diversity day or social justice day that celebrates sexual and gender diversity alongside cultural diversity.

Teachers can use the following statements and their examples to work through their attitudes and behaviours. Parents, you can give this to teachers in your children's school!

A teacher's checklist

1. I do not put down GLBT people, make jokes about them, or use jokes/hints about being GLBT to put down or control my students, or to supposedly have fun and get matey with them.

   Avoid: 'Hey Tom and Ron, you're whispering very quietly there together. Is there something we should know about you two?'

2. I use inclusive language, 'parent' instead of mother and father, 'partner' instead of 'wife' and 'husband'.

   Try: 'whoever you go into a relationship with' rather than 'when you have a boyfriend' to girls and 'when you have a girlfriend' to boys.

3. I avoid generalisations regarding gender and sexuality.

   Avoid: 'all gay men are not masculine' and 'all lesbians have short hair and play sport'.

   Try: 'There's lots of ways to be a man, and lots of ways to be gay. And there's nothing wrong with being either less muscular and feminine or being very muscular and tall.'

   'There's lots of different ways to be a lesbian. We think everyone's the same because they're the ones we see or judge as lesbian, or popular culture has made into "the lesbian". We don't recognise others and we think they're straight.'

4. I use examples in my subjects of GLBT people of diverse backgrounds with a wide range of diversity and interest.

   Try: 'Harper Lee, who wrote *To Kill a Mockingbird* about racism, later came out as a lesbian. Given she was unable to come out at a time when lesbians were seen as sick and there was no public recognition of lesbian community and culture, do you think she may have written some of her feelings about homophobia into the way she talked about racism? Hey, what about the whole plot line making Boo Radley 'come out'? Maybe there were some other things going on inside Harper Lee when she devised this character. Let's trace this character's development in the novel and see what else we may read into it now that we know this extra stuff about the author.'

You could do similar stuff with many storylines, song lyrics, poetry etc: 'Knowing that Leonard Bernstein was bisexual, what are the links to the lyrics of "Somewhere"? Do your music students know Stephen Sondheim is gay? Do they know who Walt Whitman wrote some of his poetry to? Do they know about the ongoing debates about who Shakespeare wrote his sonnets to?

Or let students into the lives of other famous people they learn about: 'Actually, for your information, John Maynard Keynes, the great economist, was bisexual, having both male and female lovers.'

Or broaden their perspective about famous events: 'When we study the Holocaust, let's not forget that there were gays, lesbians and bisexual people with pink triangles in there also getting killed. Now why do you think some history books and, yes, even some Jewish groups, try to ignore that fact?'

5. **I clarify any myths or stereotypes with facts and knowledge or I ask students to find out about the facts.**

Try: 'Actually, not all societies have seen transgender people as sick or needing to choose between being male or female. Some Native American Indian and Pacific Islander societies would be examples where they were considered sacred spiritual people with special powers. How about we look up the words "berdache" and "fa'faine", which are two names given to who we call transgender people in our society and see what we can find out.'

6. **I provide supplementary materials where it's lacking in textbooks and other resource materials.**

Try: 'This book says it's all about families but some kinds of families are missing. Here's some excerpts from a book that tells us about same-sex families and families where the parents are different sexualities. Why do you think this older textbook may not have sexually diverse families in them?'

7. **I let students know by my language and behaviour that the subjects of homosexuality, bisexuality and transgenderism can be discussed safely, seriously and comfortably around me.**

Avoid: 'I don't think your questions about sexual diversity in the animal kingdom are necessary or appropriate in my biology class. Hey class, I think he's got some kinky interest in animals!' and 'Are you trying to be disruptive by asking why the Church doesn't allow gays to get married?'

8.   I bring to the attention of other teachers and staff any homophobic language or resources they are using.

Try: 'That's a good health education resource package but it only talks about same-sex relationships in relation to STDs and HIV. I'd like to include some positive stuff about same-sex desire and relationships, and I'll find some materials for us to consider.'

Don't give up. It may not be cool for students in front of their peers to show you they support you, but something's going in. I had a particular class last year that I used to fight with because they were so homophobic. So many of the other kids were taken in by the 'cool' kids because they're quite charismatic. They're popular, so the other kids don't want to be seen to disagree. So I found it was like being up against a brick wall. I think I did bring in statistics like 10 percent of the group here will be gay and there was a sort of a shuffle about that as well. After working with one particular boy the whole year, trying to change his attitude, and thinking I got nowhere, last week he brought this other boy to me in the playground. He had come from another school and my student said to him, 'This is the best teacher in the school.' I had fought with him all year and I thought, 'Well, maybe I got something through.' His friend said, 'Oh, you're probably trying to suck up to your teacher,' and he said, 'No, I'm serious, I'm serious. This is the best teacher in the school.' **A teacher**

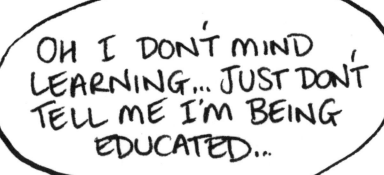

Parents' and teachers' voices are powerful voices

Adele Shaheed

You just don't tolerate homophobic comments at school. You don't tolerate them in the staff room, you don't tolerate them in your classes, and you don't tolerate them in your yard. And because my son is gay, when I'm on yard duty, I listen extra carefully and I will challenge students. And there is no need for me to say I have a gay son. I don't even say I have gay friends. I say, 'That's inappropriate. Think about it. How many of you have felt out of place [and I use that line a lot at school now] – how many times have you felt out of place, whether you were in daggy clothes on no school uniform days or whatever?' And when you challenge students like that, and you make them think, and you welcome discussion in class, it really does help.

As the student welfare coordinator in my school, I've been lucky enough to be given a room that I can equip and decorate. I've put up a lot of the PFLAG stickers, PFLAG posters. I've even had my PFLAG T-shirt on the wall from time to time. But I've tried to integrate all that material with my posters from other community services for youth, my posters from homeless associations, posters from the Drug and Alcohol Centre.

I did tell my principal that my son is gay. My principal knows both my children, and I asked if I could hang a poster in the staff room and he wouldn't let me. He wasn't comfortable with my wanting to hang that poster. I don't think he was totally comfortable with my admission, but I felt it was important to let him know. I thought it was also important that the school know my affiliation with PFLAG in case I can be used in any capacity. I let the school know that I do have people who I can contact for information.

When you hear these assumptions, come out with some realities

1. 'There are no gay people in this school. No one's ever come out.'

    'If you create an atmosphere in which every person feels safe to be themselves, you'll discover that there are GLBT students, parents and teachers as part of this community.'

2. 'The students are too young to learn about this stuff.'

    'All children need to be taught that there are many ways to live and love and be happy, about diversity and respect for "difference", about the meanings of the put-down words they're using in the school yard.'

3. 'We've got enough to handle with racism and sexism. This is too much.'

    'It should all be addressed together under social justice themes. And you know that sexism is often linked to homophobia, and that there are students from all cultures who are also GLBT. You can't slice away or forget one part of the equation of individual lives and social justice. You can't be a student or staff member in this school, protected by legislation and teaching on anti-racism, and then decide you'll turn around and hurt someone else with homophobia.'

4. 'This issue is too controversial. We don't want to alienate anyone.'

    'Human rights issues are always controversial. Have we talked to parents, teachers, students about their feelings on this and how they'd go about it? Who have you listened to that has made you worry like this? Who can we get in – from the parent groups, student groups, community groups – to support us on this work? Isn't dealing with homophobia part of what we say we do on our billboards and mission statements? I think it's controversial that we say things like "This school is a safe place for everyone," and then let it be a hard place for GLBT young people.'

5. 'Teaching about homosexuality will cause such a stir that it will interfere with the educational process in our school.'

    'Teaching about respect is fundamental to the educational process. If educators had thought like that in the past, schools would remain segregated between black and white, girls wouldn't have been allowed to undertake a broader curriculum. Education involves some stirring because it is educating and challenging the ignorance some people want to hold on to.'

6. 'This is a moral issue that our religious families will object to.'

'Yes, this is a moral issue. It is immoral to have children being hurt and abused and isolated in a school. Our religious families send their children here because we love, care and practise these values. Hatred and allowing children to be hurt are not religious values.'

7. 'If students learn about homosexuality, they'll be recruited to become homosexual. Our school will be promoting an unhealthy lifestyle.'

'Our goal is to educate students. Like all under-represented groups, GLBT students need role models, historical information, affirmation and empowerment so they can feel comfortable and loved and know they have a respected place in society. We can't "cause" homosexuality, but we can prevent suicide, depression and risk-taking behaviours. If it seems that more students begin to come out in our school, it's a sign that those students who may otherwise have been isolated or hurt or vulnerable are feeling much better about themselves. It means we're doing our job well.'

8. 'Our ethnic and migrant families will be offended as it's contrary to their cultural heritage and the maintenance of their cultural traditions, which as a multicultural school we are committed to.'

'The maintenance of discrimination, prejudice and harassment of any sort is definitely what a multicultural school is not committed to. Just as we're protecting and affirming ethnic families' children, we are here to protect and affirm all children. And isn't it racist to say that all ethnic and migrant families, and their cultural heritages, are homophobic? There are GLBT people in those cultural communities, and there are ethnic families that aren't homophobic. There are also community workers and leaders from those communities that will support our work. Let's get in touch with them and ask them to work with us so that we can be culturally sensitive and appropriate without condoning and justifying homophobic oppression.'

9. 'But this is going to need new skills. Teachers haven't got time to learn them.'

'Are new skills required? What new skills are needed? How do we handle other forms of harassment and prejudice in this school? How do we go about modifying and updating our curricula? How do we formulate and modify policies? What processes and professional expertise do we have that we use in every other facet of education and school community? What makes you think this requires strategies that are completely different and alien to us? And if there are some things we need to be updated about, there are lots of community resources and people we can call upon.'

10. 'It's irrelevant in most subjects. I don't see what sex has to do with Maths.'

'In every subject, students are making homophobic comments. In every subject, teachers can model anti-homophobic behaviour and use language that is inclusive and non-heteronormative. In every subject, there is some content, even if it's just to name a famous person who is GLBT. You asked about Maths? Well, one example is Alan Turing and his pioneering work in computer coding and cracking codes in World War Two, and how this British national hero went on to be imprisoned because he was found to be having sex with men. And this led to his suicide.'

11. 'We won't get staff consensus on this one.'

'It's rare to get consensus on any issue, but decisions have been made and actions carried through in the past because the issue was considered essential, and staff were asked to comply with it. Well, it's the same with this one.'

12. 'Parents will complain.'

'How many parents might complain? Which ones? What about parents who will support us? How much do we really know about how parents are feeling about this issue? How have we handled other issues where a vocal minority of parents have complained? What are they complaining about? What kind of work with parents needs to be done to explain what we're doing and why?'

13. 'We'll be accused of being paedophiles.'

'All the more reason to do this work. If such assumptions are held, and such fears felt, then as a school community we need to do some education about the differences between sexual diversity and paedophilia. The relationships between teachers and students are obviously being affected, which in turn affects learning and the wellbeing of our students, staff and school.'

14. 'We don't have a problem with homophobia in this school.'

'I wish this were the case and, hopefully, it will be. But at the moment, if we consider the language being used, the types of students who get bullied, the lack of GLBT content in the curriculum, and the silences around GLBT teachers, students and parents in this school community, we have a serious problem of homophobia. Let's do some research and see to what extent homophobia exists in our school.'

Our child got harassed. Even the principal treated him as if he'd just landed from outer space. We all said our bit in a meeting with the principal and asked him to take the harassment seriously. To his credit, at the end of the meeting, he got up and thanked us. His whole demeanour and attitude just changed dramatically. He said he'd been so frightened about what we might do or were going to say. **A dad**

I think parents need to find out who can be of support in the local community and school to their kids. I always want to know who my child's teachers are and if they're presenting something in a way that I can agree with or not. So I meet the teachers face to face and get a feel for who they are and what my child will be getting about GLBT issues. **A dad**

Our son came out when he was fourteen. It came to the point where he was really struggling with harassment at school, so we thought we really needed to do something about it. We went to speak to the principal, and he was great, very positive. We also made an appointment to see our other son's principal. The boys go to different schools. We wanted to let him know if there were any problems in the playground, Jess wouldn't handle it that well. He'd probably knock someone out. He said that he would make sure that there was nothing said at school about Jess's brother. Jess's school also covered sexuality in Human Relations. They spent a day a week for four weeks speaking about different relationships, straight, gay, bisexual, transgender, all that sort of thing. There were videos and discussions, which we thought was really great. So we wrote a letter to the school and said how much it meant to us that they covered the whole spectrum, not just heterosexuality. **Jan**

Is your school suffering from 'three-parent syndrome'?

Dear parents, did you know that *you* are used as the main reason why schools do not challenge homophobia and heteronormativity? Did you know that a vocal minority of parents prevent good work being done? This is TPS: three-parent syndrome. It only takes a vocal minority, about three parents, to complain about a book or program or educational practice that addresses homophobia and sexual diversity, and lots of good work gets stopped!

So become part of a vocal majority!

Speak up, act up: Let your school principals and student welfare coordinators know that you want the school to undertake sexual diversity teaching and affirmation.

Reward principals and teachers: When they undertake good practice, let them know you appreciate and support their actions by writing letters, making phone calls, attending sexual diversity events.

Address any concerns: Express your concerns regarding language used by students and teachers, and homophobic inclusions in the curriculum. Register your complaint about any homophobic harassment incident you hear about.

Become informed about equal opportunity and anti-discrimination legislation and policies: Let the school know you are informed about your legal rights as a parent and the school's legal responsibilities toward the children in its care.

Link up with other parents: Present your views and concerns, and your congratulations for good practice, as a vocal group of parents.

Reassure any GLBT teachers on staff that they have your support: Ask teachers what you can do to support their work and their own health and wellbeing.

Remember, you do not have to have a GLBT child to do all this. You do not have to 'out' your own child to do this. Insist that the school undertake its duty of care and education for all students, including yours. And remind teachers that many of them are parents too. In fact, some of them will have GLBT children. How would they want other teachers to support their children?

I made it my business to go to the school
Susan

My youngest son came out to a few teachers. I then made it my business to go up to the school and make an appointment to speak to the welfare coordinator. I wanted to support my son because things get around at school. I took heaps and heaps of written information and basically said to the welfare coordinator, 'I've had two gay children come through here, one of whom has come out while still here, so there must be more.' I suppose I was a little bit upfront but I wanted to make sure that he was looking after all the other kids that were coming through. I was stating the fact that my kids are fine because they have full support at home, but there must be other kids that are coming through with no support. I said to him, 'There's other kids here, are you helping them? Are you giving them the right information? What are you doing with them when they tell you that they're gay?'

I've had a couple of run-ins with a few teachers. I had a music teacher ring me one day. I couldn't understand what she was talking about because she was just rambling on about a song Damien's written in which he talks about being gay. I kept going, 'Oh, oh.' I wasn't saying anything because I knew where she was going, but I wasn't going to say anything until she actually said something to me. And then, in the end, she said, 'Well, is he gay?' and I said, 'Yes.' Damien was going overseas with the music group and she didn't want him to say anything about it overseas. I got angry with her and basically told her, 'Both my sons are very well adjusted and they're quite okay with the fact that they're gay. We are supportive and we prefer the fact that they are truthful to themselves and to everybody else. And if they're happy to be that way, then that's the way they're going to be and no-one else is going to change it.' I eventually got through to her, and she was very apologetic and said, 'Oh, that's fine, that's fine.'

I think teachers need to realise that you will go to the school and really give it to them, that it's okay with you that he's gay, that if he's happy, we're happy. I don't think they do an awful lot at school to fix things, but they become more comfortable with you and your children.

Another confrontation I had was with a youth worker who came up to Damien and myself in the school car park. I'd never met her before but she said, 'Oh, I need to speak to you. So and so said I must make an appointment,' and Damien and I just looked at each other.

'Well, who are you?'

'I'm the youth worker.'

'Why do we need to make an appointment?'

'Oh, because of his problem.'

'Well, what problem's that?'

'Oh, I can't really discuss it at the moment.'

'Well, who's told you to talk to us?'

'Oh, the Maths teacher.' And she named a teacher who wasn't even his Maths teacher that year. 'That was last year. What's your problem?'

'Oh, I don't know' and she left it.

So there I am thinking, 'Bloody hell! I'm sure it's about the gay thing!' So, I went to Damien's aide for his visual impairment. 'Do you know anything about this?'

'No.'

I said, 'Well I was in the paper the other day. I was interviewed about having a gay son.' And I'm thinking, I bet you it's about that.

Anyway, the youth worker rang me and she went on about Damien being isolated at school and in the end I said, 'Look, I'm not going to

Mollie Smith, Pam Garske, Narelle and Keith Phipps

get cross with you. Just tell me exactly what is the real problem?' I made an appointment to see her and I went on again, 'I've been up here before and I've got all this information here. Everything's under control with Damien but what are you doing about the other kids?' She rang me back later and said, 'Oh, I really do need to apologise to you.'

'Oh, why is that?'

'The teacher was talking about someone else.'

I actually laughed and said, 'So why did you think it was Damien?'

'Because he's gay.'

So because he was openly gay, she automatically thought he'd be having problems. But after that, she began to give out information, and took more information from us.

Gillian Maury (far right) with her mum, her three children and their partners

Parents teaching schools

PFLAG groups are international, state and regional parent groups that support the parents, families and friends of GLBT young people. They're also there to act as advocates and activists in your schools and communities. Invite PFLAG parents in to work with you in your school. They can talk to student groups, at parent nights, and be part of teachers' professional development sessions. Check out the back of this book for your local PFLAG group. And if there isn't one, it's time there was! Contact your nearest PFLAG group and they'll help you get started.

Let's hear from two PFLAG mums.

My son prayed to be normal
Karen Stuart

I believe teachers should be given opportunities through in-service days to learn about homosexuality, homophobia and their responsibilities as teachers. My own son said he used to pray to God at night that he could be 'normal' – should any twelve-year-old have to feel that way?

I give talks to teachers and students in schools about being a mother of a gay son. This is the sort of stuff we need to see done more in schools. When I speak to students, I start off about being a parent and having three children, two boys and a girl, and how each of the children is different, and then I gradually talk about how one of my sons told me he was gay. They're always terribly, terribly interested. One of the main things boys are always interested in is, 'Oh, how did his father take it? How was his dad?'

I've been giving that talk for about five years. At one session, I had a male teacher come up to me. He's got three young sons and he said that by listening to me talk, he really thought about his own three boys. Perhaps one of them could grow up to be gay.

Bigots are not born

Nan McGregor

When my son Kieran came out to his father and to me, I felt shocked and betrayed, not by the knowledge of his gayness, but by the knowledge that for the final three years of his secondary education at a Catholic boys' school, he'd been systematically bullied and harassed. From the early morning classes to the end of his school day he was victimised. He was punched, he was spat on, he was ridiculed simply because some people within that school community decided that he deserved to be punished, simply for being himself.

In my involvement with PFLAG I've heard similar stories far too often. Stories of young people like my son who toughened himself and weathered the storms of what were supposed to be the best years of his life, stories of others who simply gave up, who either had their education curtailed or postponed, who had to transfer to other schools, or who decided that the burden was far too heavy and who chose to end their lives. Far too often, I've heard parents at a PFLAG meeting conclude statements about their GLBT children with an almost throw-away remark, 'Of course, he/she had a most miserable time at school … '. The mere notion that school was not a caring and nurturing environment for the young person is something which I find most offensive.

Although I can't understand why such bullying occurs, I'm convinced that bigots are not born, but that they adopt the attitudes and ideas of their particular environment. I hope that schools will adopt policies that attack homophobic bullying, whether that bullying is through the use of derogatory words, or physical violence. Protection of 'out' students is vital but protection must also be extended towards those students whom it's assumed may be GLBT, and to any students who may have a GLBT parent/s or sibling. Any information sheets for parents or school prospectus statements should make parents aware that the school will not tolerate any form of bullying including homophobic bullying. Students, also, should be made aware that any form of homophobic bullying is not acceptable and will be dealt with.

Parents should demand that these issues be addressed, and the rights of GLBT pupils be protected. Groups like PFLAG can lobby schools to provide personal, social and sexuality education which affirm the existence of GLBT young people. Education should be available which provides young people with accurate information about the diversity of adult GLBT life. PFLAG can send brochures and speakers to schools, and promote the need for training of people who work with children and adolescents.

PFLAG parents want all students, including their own children, to be educated in a safe and secure environment.

(l. to r.) Nan McGregor, Karen Stuart and (seated) A/Sergeant Melinda Edwards of the Victorian Police Gay and Lesbian Unit

Challenge the 'blame the victim' approach

One of the issues many parents and GLBT youth talk to me about is how schools may adopt the 'blame the victim' approach. In other words, aspects or traits of a young person, or the very being GLBT itself, may be seen as the problem. Questions get asked like, 'So what do you think you did to bring on this harassment?' Comments, disguised as 'helpful hints', get made such as, 'What if you lowered your voice a little? What if you didn't move your arms around so much?' (to boys) and 'What if you put on some make-up, grew your hair, and wore a dress to the prom? What if you weren't so loud in class?' (to girls). The intention of such comments, often made by parents as well, may be to protect your child, but it reinforces their feeling that ultimately something's wrong with them.

As parents, insist that the school focuses on what the problem really is. Not your child's individuality, sexuality or way of doing gender, but the narrow-mindedness, conformity and bigotry in other children and within the school system regarding sexual and gender diversity. Don't allow the issues to be minimised or dismissed with comments like, 'boys will be boys', 'everyone gets teased about something', 'they have to learn to handle these things'.

If a GLBT child is being passively resistant or aggressively disruptive, a 'behaviour management problem', the school needs to ask why. What frustrations and situations may have led to this? And this is not about excusing or justifying inappropriate behaviour in GLBT children (remember, no pedestal!), but about working out what other 'inappropriate behaviour' toward your child is being excused or justified.

Have a listen to mother and daughter team, Leanne and Sandra, as they tell us about their experiences in dealing with a school's 'blame the victim' approach.

How much cruelty do we feel comfortable with?

Sandra and Leanne

Sandra: Every day I get harassed. People constantly stare at me trying to figure out if I'm a boy or a girl ... in some faces I see disgust and often hatred. This makes me feel very insecure and anti-social. I've been in numerous situations where I've had to physically defend myself. Additionally I've

Leanne: I'm not advocating special rights for some kids ... I'm here as a parent to say all kids should be given the same rights, the right to adequately resourced services, to attend school in safety, to support and recognition when needing help and, more importantly, the right to be treated with

been shouted at and called every degrading name you could possibly imagine. I don't understand why it happens. Everyone has feelings and when you have what feels like an entire world constantly degrading you, you do start to question your whole self-worth as a person. Often it's kind of like living two lives. Some days I get to the point when I just can't take any more.

When I was in primary school I didn't have the faintest idea of what a lesbian was. So when I started to find myself attracted to girls I thought I had a disease. I hung around mainly with the boys regardless that I was often banned from some of their games because some considered that girls just shouldn't be playing like that. This led to me being labelled a tomboy. Sometimes I'd start to think, 'Well what sort of stuff do girls do? Should I be doing that kind of stuff?' Mostly I felt very isolated and alone.

High school came and brought with it a lot of difficulties. I remember all the girls could ever talk about was the guys. I couldn't stop thinking about the girls. I couldn't tell anyone how I was really feeling mainly out of fear for my safety so a really horrible war began inside of me. There was no information about people

respect and dignity.

Sandra's been labelled among other things a freak, a sexual predator, a perverted person, and told she's not normal. To watch with tremendous pride in her achievements but to also fear for her emotional and physical safety on a daily basis is something of a strain and concern to say the least. Not just to see her experience victimisation at the hands of her peers but additionally at the hands of ill-informed adults … These were hard times for us.

Sandra was diagnosed as having ADD along with depression. She was automatically medicated with dextroamphetamine and antidepressants. This all at the age of fifteen. Several times, I raised with her specialist the issue of her experiencing problems surrounding her sexuality. Her specialist's advice was, 'It's probably only a phase, she'll grow out of it, and from experience in treating adolescent girls with ADD, a lot do present with a butch or masculine image.' Well, however experienced this specialist is, however well meaning this advice was, it was an incorrect diagnosis of my child. All the abuse and harassment resulted in Sandra feeling embarrassed, and reducing her to a defensive hostile state.

like myself at school so I didn't really get any help. I felt really alone and very, very angry.

I fell into a state of depression and started to become self-abusive. I was filled with a lot of anger toward myself and everyone around me. I got into a lot of fights and although I take responsibility for my actions, I also think that the education system and some of our support services had their own part that they played too by not offering me the assistance that I tried to seek out and desperately needed at this stage.

I was forced out of a high school that was at the back of my house to another school that I had to travel to two hours a day by bus. This school seemed a little more tolerant at first. I think because it was an all girls school, but again I became victimised there too. I had one person who actually tried to stab me with a pair of scissors, another group who beat me, then hit me continually with a metal garbage can, and a teacher at this school who felt it was his right and duty to make me out as a sexual predator. I tried to escape school by staying in the counsellor's office, visiting him about four times a week, but even he couldn't figure out why this was happening.

After a chain of events at school, Sandra's education was cut short at fifteen. We had no choice but to remove her from the school environment. When you request to speak with a particular teacher regarding your daughter being publicly maligned and brutalised, only to be issued with a message sent by this teacher refusing any discussion with you until they can arrange for a union rep to accompany them, you start to wonder. Eventually a discussion resembling something like the Mad Hatter's Tea Party took place. It included the teacher in question, the school principal, the school counsellor and private legal representation on our daughter's behalf. This teacher's sole justification for their actions was that they felt Sandra wasn't a good role model. Regardless that this claim was proven to be unsupported and unfounded, there wasn't even an apology. I ask: What sort of role model is this teacher to students at that school, considering their actions were blatantly discriminatory and indeed illegal?

How much cruelty do we expect some kids to endure as part of their growing? How much cruelty do we feel comfortable with? So the birth of change will

Through my family's endless searching, the first place I was really ever accepted was at a young GLBT support group. There I was treated just like every one else. There my many other talents as a person were recognised and encouraged. I also attend PFLAG meetings with my mum and it's here that people have something positive to offer to everybody.

I've got to where I am today with the unconditional love and understanding from my family and the groups I mentioned, along with a terrific adolescent counsellor. More importantly I give myself the credit for having the courage to always be who I am and to forever stand with pride.

begin with us being uncomfortable, challenging current systems and ideas, so obviously narrow and soul destroying to many.

How many of you, if visiting a new place, would navigate your way around using maps that were outdated and published years ago? What would happen? Well, many of you would become lost, disorientated, blind, even miss seeing some magnificent places. Why? Because your old map couldn't possibly show the information needed to get to these new places. It wouldn't show that some streets had been closed, entire new suburbs had been created. Let's start to update our geographics of life so that we can begin to navigate our way to discover and learn the areas that may seem unfamiliar.

If it takes many ingredients to make one perfect thing then these kids are all one important ingredient in the recipe of one perfect thing: humanity.

I had one teacher who was quite nasty to me in front of another one of his classes. I thought I'd left my bag in there from the class before, and he was rude and aloof about it. He then turned to some favourite students of his in the class and said, 'Oh, sorry about that, I'm homophobic,' as a joke. I took some violent action toward him. I didn't take it lying down. I realise it wasn't the best way to handle it, but I was so angry. **YGLAM Youth Group member**

Invite GLBT young people to speak at your school! Madelaine and Luciano talk about the work they do in schools, as well as providing examples of the kinds of responses they get.

OUTSpoken: students speaking out

Madelaine and Luciano

OUT of frustration: We decided to form the group widely known as OUTSpoken because there seemed to be an invisibility of 'out' GLBT students in schools. This was so evident in the private schools we attended.

Luc: I walked to my locker in the corridor with my head still tangled after what seemed like a whole day of algebra but was, in fact, barely an hour. I saw him coming but decided I couldn't be bothered worrying about it, the consistent dread of teasing. Sticks and stones did break my bones, but the fact was that words didn't really bother me.

In the hierarchy of Year 11, he was classified as 'cool'. He gained this status from constantly tormenting those he thought to be a lesser 'man' than himself, like maybe my friend Peter with the glasses, or Phil the computer nerd, or me, the gay guy. There was nothing particularly different about this day. I'd been called a fag enough times to have gotten completely used to it and brush it off accordingly.

'Here comes the fag!' he shouted across the corridor.

I rolled my eyes at the sheer stupidity of the sound of his voice. As I walked away, anger came over me and I walked to my next class frustrated and annoyed.

When I got home that day I realised that while his name-calling was boring and unoriginal, it was also completely unjust. I'd done nothing to deserve anything like that and neither had the guy down the street who'd been bashed for supposedly being gay. And so I dropped my schoolbag, sat at my desk and wrote away furiously. Someone had to know that this wasn't acceptable.

I signed my letter 'Angry Senior Student', sealed it and wrote on it the destination – a GLBT community newspaper, the only method I knew to make myself heard and contact others that were feeling the same frustration as I was.

Madelaine: The students were baffled by the anonymous letter in the student rag. Who was 'queer' in their safe, sheltered private school? Which student would write about being gay anyway? It was asking for crucifixion.

I needed to say something. I needed my fellow students to know that I suffered every time they joked about gays and lesbians. That my 'straight' front was about to be busted, and they would all know the secret I was trying desperately to hide. I was slowly coming to terms with my own sexuality, and I needed a safer environment in which to express myself and my individuality. An anonymous letter was as close as I could I get to expressing myself.

After this, I began to feel more comfortable with my sexuality, and I told a supposedly accepting classmate that I was the anonymous student. She was supportive, until she told the whole cast and crew of the school musical. I was devastated, and angry. It was like I was moving forward, then physically being thrown back. Along with feeling frustrated and violated, I began to feel the injustice – of being outed and of being vilified for my sexuality.

One lunchtime, I went down to an inner city street which many GLBT people frequented, to get away from it all. Picking up a GLBT newspaper, I sat and read every word, taking in as much of the gay community as I could: it was the only sanctuary I had. Reading the letters page, I read one from someone signing 'Angry Senior Student' that spoke everything that I was feeling. I was angry too, and felt just as powerless and frustrated. Later that day, gripped by the same power-lessness of that angry student, I wrote my reply and so started the chain of events that led to OUTSpoken.

'Education is the key to change and you should be proud you are a part of it!!'

As out and proud students going into schools, not only do we have the benefit of our own experiences of discrimination at school, we are students ourselves. We felt this was a vital point, and we'd have a greater impact by talking to students as students.

OUTThere/OUTLandish: Through many avenues, we were able to form a contact network. From this, we gained a name for ourselves and were approached by many interested educationalists who were heartened by the rise of a gay and lesbian youth group run solely by students for students.

'I learnt a lot. Not having a lot to do with gay people, it was really interesting hearing different people's opinions on aspects of homosexuality.'

We did not wish to appear as 'exhibit A' and 'exhibit B', yet there seemed to be no other way to put a human face to 'faggots' and 'dykes'. We were also aware that, statistically, in every class there may be same-sex attracted students who were questioning their own sexuality. If we could help just one of these students – either to affirm themselves or stop their classmates' lack of understanding – then OUTSpoken would have achieved its primary aim.

'At the start I felt a bit uncomfortable with you talking about it [homosexuality], but as the session went on I became comfortable enough to mention my gay sister.'

Speaking OUT/Breaking OUT: Our first invitation came from Clare Lyons, a Religion and Society teacher. As we approached the date of our very first 'class', we found ourselves becoming quite nervous and realising that it wasn't going to be as easy as we'd first thought.

However, the more active we became over time and the more we interacted with students from schools and universities, the clearer the structure of our presentations became.

We begin each class with a disclaimer, stating that we feel we shouldn't have to be in front of a class of students talking about homosexuality and heterosexism: it's really quite unfortunate and reflects on the state of the broader community and its lack of ability to embrace diversity. A group like OUTSpoken shouldn't be necessary. So in the end, we wish to make our sessions redundant.

'I learnt that you guys are so much like every other member of the community, and that it is pathetic how the majority of society don't regard you in that way.'

After the disclaimer, we make it clear what perspective we'll take in the class. We are honest with the students, and expect the same in return. OUTSpoken talks about our own experiences from a gay man and lesbian woman's perspective. While we try to cover bisexual and transgender issues, we also realise that we can't speak with the voice of these identities. Therefore, we include these issues as objectively as possible, so as not to marginalise the marginalised.

'The session was fantastic. The more you can educate, the more people can begin to understand ... '

Before group discussions, we introduce ourselves to the group and speak on various issues such as educational policy, religion, health, safe sex, and media representations. Depending on the circumstances and the brief we are given by the facilitator of the group, our focus varies. Students always seem to move away from any academic topic and want to focus more on 'real life stuff' such as our coming out stories and the reactions of family and friends. We talk about things we share in common with other students: we have love dramas, trouble getting our homework done, problems with our parents.

'I think it's important to give your side of the story. I also think it's important to talk about the reactions of your family and friends.'

We've come to learn some strategies that help facilitate open and honest discussions, where people feel free to express their opinions without fear of recrimination. Clearly, many students have strong ideas and opinions that conflict with other students and sometimes teachers and facilitators. We believe these ideas need to be spoken, in a respectful manner, rather than fester unspoken and unacknowledged.

'I did not agree on some things discussed, but that makes for good discussion.'

We've come across homophobic students. In open and frank discussion with us and their classmates, they've seen the 'other side' of the coin, often surprisingly held up to them by their closest friends. Being free to voice themselves has allowed many myths and fallacies to be shattered, and many students' eyes to be opened to diversity.

'The speakers made me realise that there is a lot more to discrimination than I previously thought.'

We often ask students to look at stereotypes of homosexuality, generational differences and some scenarios that the students may experience at some point in their lives. For example, we ask them to put themselves in a situation where they have a GLBT doctor, brother, mother, school friend, and consider how they would react.

Another important issue we cover is the reaction from both teachers and students within our own schools. It's easy for a student brought up in a relatively conservative culture to submit to the overwhelming homophobia around them, brushing it off as a normal part of school life.

'I do feel more comfortable about it all ... your session sort of helped with my sexuality as well ... your stories touched me ... it was humorous and beautiful.'

Very rarely have we come across a group that hasn't jumped at the opportunity to ask us questions and discuss the issues raised. Indeed, in many classes we've spent over an hour in heated discussion and debate and, often, students have veered off in a different direction by wanting to talk about things that we may not have covered directly. We're constantly surprised about the tangents students wish to take on – anything from butch–femme relationships to gay and lesbian parenting. It seems clear to us that there's an expanse of issues that students wish to cover and with which they're fascinated and intrigued, but that they wouldn't usually feel comfortable bringing up in your everyday school situation. Teachers have said that for weeks following our class, the issues that we touched on and others springing from our session have come up and launched more discussion, even in unrelated classes.

Finally ... why OUT, why bother?

Luc: I began my activism at school when I realised that there were other problems in our world besides dealing with drugs and racism. Not to detract from the importance of making sure those things are also dealt with, I felt that homophobia was not addressed at all and that GLBT people just didn't exist to my fellow students and teachers. I approached school chaplains and put the issue to them – my 'complaining', as it was called, went largely unnoticed till I outed myself at fifteen.

After much discussion with the relevant people, a unit of homophobia was introduced into our Ethics course. Finally, I felt as if I'd achieved something. However, reactions by fellow students were what I'd expected them to be.

I kept at it, writing things for the school newspaper and practically jumping on someone when I heard homophobic comments in the corridors. By the end of my final year, however, I reflected on the changes I'd made to my school with a certain amount of pride. People knew about me and for the large part, student attitudes had gone from disgusted to tolerant, which is more than I could've hoped for.

My family were a huge source of support for me – something I was originally shocked at because of the general attitude of other Italian Catholic parents. My family's support, together with the belief that not all people are bullies, was my driving force in investing time and effort into OUTSpoken.

Madelaine: My first act of 'queer activism' was to write in the school paper. Eventually, I edited this paper and attempted to ensure that there was a fair representation of non-heterosexual identities. This was a difficult task, but the process felt as important as the outcomes. Just standing up and being visible was a huge step in the right direction. Saying that GLBT students are on campus, not just on TV or a Pride March, was a surprisingly potent step – students and staff began to see that this wasn't something that just happened elsewhere. Gays and lesbians exist, they exist as students, teachers and parents. Our aim is to appear as part of a diverse multifaceted society which includes lesbians and gays.

The feedback we've had from students, staff and the community has been overwhelmingly positive. The fact that we're still doing this after seven years is a testament to that, and we believe that the days when this all seems irrelevant are nearing.

'Thank you. You gave me inspiration. Last night, I told my mother that I'm gay.'

Madelaine and Luciano

OUTSpoken: teachers speaking out
Clare Lyons

On a warm Wednesday in September my friend's ashen face told me something awful had happened. Soon the news was all around the school as the horror of an ex-student's suicide became known. Who knows why he killed himself … but that he had suffered homophobic harassment, I believe, just had to have had some impact on his level of resilience to the other issues of life. The insidious power of harassment to remain hidden from staff enabled James's bullies to continue and – when he died – led to many accusations that the school hadn't fulfilled its duty of care adequately.

Ironically, it often takes tragedy to occur to enable words to be spoken and actions to be taken on behalf of those who have no voice. In discerning how to respond to James's tragic death, some of us on staff planned a staff meeting session to raise awareness of the fact that some students are at risk. Loners, the socially unaccepted, those students with learning difficulties or those who are gifted, GLBT students, those with disability – all at risk of isolation and its effects, the most extreme of which is successful suicide.

I felt that educating staff was one thing, but that students needed to be given an opportunity to face their own homophobia. I chose to offer my Religion and Society students a unit of work on homosexuality, part of which was my request to OUTSpoken to come to our school, meet and address our students. After the session, one student who's gay himself, realised that 'many of my peers were more

Clare Lyons and her boys

accepting than I thought' and was grateful that the session 'opened the door to a lot of new discussions'. While this student was not out himself, the session allowed him some element of feeling more positive and less isolated among his peers. A telling remark from another student: 'I was amazed at the hell gay people go through. I guess I never really thought about how they themselves would have to deal with it.'

Meeting Madelaine and Luciano was a wonderful experience for my students. Many students made comments like the following: 'the speakers have the integrity, courage to speak from their hearts and as human beings crying out from a disgraceful oppression ... you guys made my week'.

Both at that time and since, various people have asked me how it was that a Catholic school welcomed openly gay young people to speak to its students, given the Church's and Catholic education system's public stance on homosexuality. A second question has usually been 'Weren't you afraid of the consequences?', implying that my own teaching career might suffer if I was too proactive. In the Hebrew Scriptures, Queen Esther, pondering the advice of Mordecai, 'if you keep silent at such a time as this ...', risked being outed as a Jew to protect her people against the evil Haman. Jewish people have a saying that to save one life is to redeem the whole world – a task for all of us, gay and straight – for the evil of Haman is with us still. Schools can only speak out if teachers are willing to be their voice. In my more fragile moments, I do fear the consequences, yet I have to keep reminding myself that that fear itself is the very thing that keeps so many people silent in the face of the frequent 'gay agenda' catch-cry. The OUTSpoken session was a positive, non-threatening way to offer students and staff some release from their own cultural captivity.

Encouraging other teachers to become OUTSpoken:
At the 'Students at Risk' staff in-service, I was asked to address the issue of GLBT students. I firmly believe that we carry – literally – our experiences in our bodies, hence expressions such as 'pain in the neck', 'get off my back', 'shouldering one's burden'. So as I reflected on what to say to my colleagues, I decided that the best way for them to understand what some GLBT kids go through is to go through it themselves. I designed the following exercise in the hope that they could really know in their bones as some GLBT kids know.

Teeth

I know that having teeth is not a nice thing, and – thank God – no-one in this room does have teeth. (Here I pause in order for their reaction – laughter, queries whether they had heard right, etc. I keep a very [pardon the pun] straight and serious face. Continuing I say:) *But I'd like you to pretend that you are blighted with teeth … I apologise if this offends your sensibilities.*

In pairs, I'd ask you to speak to each other, but in such a way, of course, that your shameful secret is not found out – the other person must not see that you have teeth. You have one minute.

(Before the minute's up, the noise level in the room has decreased considerably, and many pairs have given up.)

Any comments? What happened in your bodies?

(Responses include: I didn't want to look them in the eye, I felt ashamed, I couldn't express myself, my face and shoulders were tense, I didn't say anything, I chose not to participate, I limited myself to saying only what I had to say, I felt the other person didn't really see me, I felt that I was hiding and I felt guilty.

Once these responses have been given, I continue.)

For our GLBT students, this is the effort they must put in every day to keep their cover, or to deflect the harassment they cop in a homophobic school. Unlike other harassed kids who can go home to safe and accepting families, gay kids often have to keep up the pretence at home as well.

(Pause)

Sexuality is fundamental to identity. Yet for GLBT kids, harassment and shame erode the soul, leaving little solidity on which to base a life. How our gay kids have any energy left for the other issues of life, after putting up with such cruelty, I don't know.

Schools exist to invite young people to take hold of life, not to encourage them to let it go. Homophobia does kill. The issue of homophobia has to start with us as a staff – if we supposedly intelligent people are afraid of being gay-friendly in case people think we are gay, and if we allow homophobia in our classrooms or our staffrooms, we are taking our part in supporting youth suicide.

(During this last part, there's a palpable sense of people listening intently. When I pause at the end and then start towards my seat, I think: They now know something on a level they haven't known before.)

Teachers working with OUTSpoken parents: For staff in many school communities, there's always an experience of walking that fine line between proactive care for students, and keeping diplomatic peace between the school and parents. Such a journey is not always easy, and can be daunting; the temptation to give in because it's all too hard is frequent. What is essential for minority students – and particularly for GLBT students – is that staff keep 'nipping away' at the heels of heterosexism and fundamentalism that rob these students of their right to safety, sexuality education, respect and affirmation of them as esteemed members of their school communities. Such work is at times particularly tiresome in schools administered in the name of churches.

However, the Catholic Church for example, teaches that homosexuals 'must be accepted with respect, compassion and sensitivity. Every sign of unjust discrimination in their regard should be avoided.' (*Catechism of the Catholic Church 1994*, par. 2358). This gives a clear mandate to teachers in Catholic schools to work proactively to educate their students. The important thing to note here though is that many people do not know – nor accept – the teaching.

The following parent–teacher interview scenario is based on personal experience and provides an example of how to respond to parental anger at sexual diversity teaching in a Catholic school:

Parent: I find it disgraceful that a Catholic school would do the topic of homosexuality. My daughter's been asked to fill in a questionnaire, 'Are you homophobic?' and to prepare a role-play which asked them to pretend the majority of people were gay and that they were straight and had to 'come out' to a significant other person. Why are you doing such a thing?

Teacher: Well, the Church teaches that homosexuals must be accepted with respect, compassion and sensitivity and that no unjust prejudice is to be shown in their regard.

Parent: That's not Church teaching.

Teacher: Yes, it is. Its source is the Catechism of the Catholic Church.

Parent: What church? That's not the teaching of my church.

Teacher: Well, Pope John Paul II oversaw the publication of the Catechism and it conveyed the authoritative teachings of the Roman Catholic Church.

Parent: You must be misrepresenting Church teaching.

Teacher: No, I'm quoting word for word from the Catechism – verbatim.

Parent: Last night I wrote to the Archbishop to complain. He wouldn't give gay people communion.

Teacher: That's a different issue. As the person responsible for Religious Education at a Catholic school I have to ensure that our students know what the Church teaches, and this teaching is important because of the widespread occurrence of homophobia. Suicidality research reports that gay youth are seven times more likely to attempt suicide.

Parent: How do you know this?

Teacher: I've read the research; we have a duty to ensure that none of our students are at risk, and gay students are at greater risk of suiciding.

Parent: Well they should kill themselves.

Teacher: I find it abhorrent that any Catholic would want another person dead, and that is absolutely against any Church teaching.

Parent: As parents we work hard to raise our children and to teach them their religion and we do not appreciate you putting students here at risk of becoming homosexual.

Teacher: Research shows that most people do not choose their sexual orientation, and the Catholic Church also teaches that in the Catechism. Research shows that the great majority of people's sexual orientation is clear to them by the time they're in mid-secondary school. Would you like me to send you a copy of the Catechism's teaching on homosexuality, and a copy of the section from the textbook?

Parent: If you want to.

Teacher: Thank you for coming today.

This dialogue shows the importance of teachers knowing the ground on which they stand and handling any interview with parents professionally and calmly (even though quoting research and other resources makes little difference to someone's personal belief system in this area). Within the present culture of the Catholic Church, it's vital that teachers know what the Church teaches so that they are not bullied into doing nothing by parents like the one above. It is true that the Catholic Church does not accept homosexual relationships, but the teaching about respect, compassion, sensitivity and lack of prejudice is not directed to homosexual Catholics; it is an imperative addressed to the entire church. This teaching is more important than that addressed to homosexuals, especially as if it is 'obeyed' it will affirm GLBT students and acknowledge them as equal members of every Catholic school community.

Challenge the 'ethnic excuse'

I've already talked about 'parents who complain' as being the main excuse schools will use for not challenging homophobia and heteronormativity. Well, what I call the 'ethnic excuse' is another main one. This is the line that any anti-homophobic work will upset the ethnic parents, be seen as racist, and is against the promotion of multiculturalism in the school.

Let's hear from Lian who takes us into how many students in our schools are negotiating their interwoven realities of ethnicity, gender and sexuality, and how the school can play a major role in supporting culturally diverse young people to connect with their sexualities and ethnicities.

'Constant cravings' in high school
Lian Low

While I was in high school, the curtains in my bedroom were always drawn and the room dark. I didn't have to know about the world outside my window if I didn't want to. The world outside my door had too many angry and sad voices – echoes of uprooted displacement – of being in a foreign land and not knowing its vernacular. My friends thought I was weird cos I liked kd lang's daggy music. My mum caught a glimpse of my playback of 'Hush Sweet Lover' on one of my accidental off-guard days, and thought kd was male, and Asian.

I was fourteen when I arrived in Australia. I had long hair, which I kept till the second year of uni because it was my mask. I'm of Straits Chinese-Malaysian background. The first day in high school the people who came up and talked to me were two Asian girls. One who was from Hong Kong and the other one of Vietnamese background. My core group of friends were mostly of Asian background – Singapore included. Most of them were girls, some boys. Most of us (except two) did English language classes (even though the classes bored me shitless), and all of us together comprised the 'Asian' group in our year level.

I was used to the experience of having 'respect' for people from older year levels, or who were older than me. But at this high school, I felt like everyone could walk over me. I remember racist taunts from kids in younger levels. Perhaps it had something to do with how well we spoke English, how well we understood it. Perhaps it had something to do with how we wore our school uniform, what we ate for lunch, who we hung out with … Maybe petty stuff, maybe something about how we all had yellowy tinges to our skin, how some of us spoke funny languages, and we didn't really look any different from each other, really. Who knows?

Multiculturalism was in at the time. The school system offered us students the staple of one meat (Shakespeare – who else?) and the 'optional' three veg. (often an open miscellaneous category – depending on the whim of the school board – ranging from Thomas Hardy to Jack Davies). The education system was so obviously patriarchal, middle-class, Anglo- and hetero-centric. I thought that was normal – I was getting a 'good' education. You don't really think of questioning the System when you're in it. When what's rammed into your head is – Study! Study! Study! – Get into Uni. The best one. Otherwise you'll never get a good job. Ho-hum.

The idea of coming out at high school wasn't a question that I entertained. I don't think I knew what coming out meant. Now, after four years of being 'out' (officially) and meeting other womyn 'like me', whether through a common language of sexuality, or sexuality and ethnicity, has enabled me to see that my gender, my skin colour, my culture and my sexuality are intertwined. My sexuality and my ethnicity should not have to be compartmentalised into separate worlds. In reality when they do unavoidably collide (e.g. lunch with parents and brother in an Italian restaurant and dyke couple that I know sitting opposite) I feel disoriented. Who am I now? Am I : Asian (i.e. Straits Chinese-Malaysian background)? Lesbian? (I had the impression that *all* dykes were *mostly* 'White' and *all* drank alcohol). Or Womyn? (Only stupid ugly men call womyn 'girls'.)

I can write flippantly and laugh a little now at my 'angst' while I was at school. But it makes me angry that it was 'normal' to have those years fraught with depression, loneliness and anxiety. It's even more difficult when you feel alienated from your family and there are societal pressures and norms that silence you – regardless of cultural and/or racial background or identity.

I wish that I'd had access to material and resources that reflected who I was at high school. I wish that I didn't have to think that I was the only one who was going through all this. I know now that it isn't my fault that I didn't. What I had around me was what was available and accessible to me. I wish schools were open to showing films like *Show Me Love*, *Only The Brave*, *Incredibly True Adventures of Two Girls In Love*, and *Fire*. Audre Lorde, Adrienne Rich, and other GLBT writers, especially ethnic, Indigenous and Black GLBT writers should be read. Multicultural GLBT collections such as *Inside Out – Coming Out Stories, The Very Inside: An Anthology of Asian Pacific-Islander Lesbian and Bisexual Women, This Bridge Called My Back: Writings By Radical Women of Color, Amazon to Zami: Towards a Global Lesbian Feminism, Zami: A New Spelling of My Name* and *Multicultural Queer: Australian Narratives* should be on the school syllabus, if not on the library shelves.

High school is one of our most formative environments. Either the system changes, or with networking and resources, we change the system. Sometimes the 'softly, softly' approach is too subtle because schools take too much of a conservative middle ground. Sometimes you have to scream and shout, protest and dissent, to fight for your rights. And when you do, you'll be surprised that you're not the only one.

Challenge the 'gender binary'

There are children in our schools who do not fit neatly and absolutely into the socio-scientific categories of 'male' and 'female'. As Jacqui Cussen writes in the following contribution, our schools, indeed our societies, need to make room for gender diversity rather than enforce 'gender duality'.

Not fitting the gender binary doesn't make you a monster

Jacqui Zephyr Cussen

If you teach a transgender student you'll probably never know it. It might not be the girl who displays masculine behaviours and is perhaps not the boy who plays only with girls.

Transgendered children learn very early that they're safest in keeping that truth very well hidden. Children understand that belonging and being accepted are crucial to survival. They learn where they are meant to take their place and the painful consequences inflicted by parents and peers if they try to cross gender boundaries. Our education system reinforces this vigorously. We understand well the ways these boundaries limit and restrict individual children. We do not dispute the need for girls to be able to attempt, fail and succeed at activities traditionally

Jacqui Cussen

accessible only to boys and we encourage girls and boys to engage in a range of activities to empower them in making life choices.

We put up barriers, however, when a child says that they wish to inhabit a different place in the gender landscape. There is no place for a child who wants to be both a girl and a boy, nor is there room for one who wants to be neither, nor for the child who wishes to alternate, or for the child who has been wrongly classified. Children know themselves and it's foolish of us to imagine we can force them into a mould without damaging them. To include and protect this most marginalised and disempowered group we must educate ourselves to avoid isolating transgendered children any further.

Transgendered students are not going to pull you up and say, 'Hey, stop excluding me.' The issue will remain hidden. That is, until you screen *Priscilla, Queen of the Desert*. Teachers can use it as a class text and there are many support materials available. However, not everyone seems to realise that only two of the three travellers are drag queens. The third, Terence Stamp's character, is a pre-operative male-to-female transgendered person. Enjoyable as the film is for its comic escapism, some of the stereotypes it presents might be misleading, especially if they're the only images available to students or if we, as teachers, are unable to sufficiently deconstruct the characters. The representation of Asian women is a stark example, but one which teachers are hopefully well equipped to deconstruct and analyse.

I would not for a moment suggest that we avoid *Priscilla* simply because it deals in stereotypes. Any opportunity to critically analyse social representations and explore the full spectrum of genders is to be grasped. However alternative images of transgenderism are available for comparison in anthologies of autobiographical accounts. Other films to consider include the 1998 French film, *Ma Vie en Rose*, which portrays the life of a child who adopts so-called 'gender-inappropriate' behaviours and the isolation and punishment subsequently inflicted. *La Nuit des Etoiles* is another movie providing a well-developed transgender character. A Canadian–French collaboration (in English), it tells of a girl meeting her transgender father after some years' separation. Radclyffe Hall, noted lesbian author from the early part of last century, presents a complex female-to-male transgender in her novel, *The Well of Loneliness*. Excerpts from these and other texts could be examined. Other resources that might be used to guide your own research, but which as 'R' rated films may not be suited to screening in full in class, include *Boys Don't Cry* and *The Crying Game*. However, appropriate excerpts from these films may be very useful.

By presenting these alternative images it would become possible to empower all students to recognise the broad range of gender presentations that people adopt, thus equipping them with a greater social ability. It also provides an opportunity for those hidden students who live outside society's boundaries of two genders to see that there are options available to them. It would show those children that not fitting the girl or boy, woman or man model does not make you a monster.

Creating a safe classroom, one in which those who are differently gendered can feel they belong, can be done. One of the ways in which a safe environment can be created is by adjusting the way students are divided into groups. It is simple to avoid exclusion even when grouping into genders. Invite students to arrange into three groups, those who wish to be in the girls' group, those who wish to be in the boys' group, and those who wish to be in a mixed group. For almost any activity, this offers the opportunity for students to determine their own place. Those who are differently gendered have the chance to go where they want to belong (if they are that confident) or to join the mixed group, thus freeing them from inappropriate classification and avoiding exposing them to ridicule or danger.

If you teach a transgender student you will probably never know it, but the student will. Unless we make schools safe for transgender students many will continue to see suicide and risk-taking behaviours such as drug-taking as best available options. The very best first step is to demystify transgenderism, to accept that it's real, that it's not an illness to be cured, a deviance to be punished, an explanation for bullying, nor a reason for exclusion.

I had long conversations with Jess, my transteen, about what could happen if he wore so-called girls' clothes at school. It's about explaining that you understand that it feels right and it definitely is right for them to dress as they want and be the gender they feel they are, but that their safety is important too. Because school isn't a safe place for Jess to explore his femininity, I made my home a safe haven for him to be a young woman. I also got Jess in touch with local groups and places where being a transteen wasn't an issue. **Roberta**

Challenge the 'sexual binary'

If we take up Jacqui Cussen's reflections on gender diversity and apply them to bisexual young people, we can see that not fitting the 'sexual binary' also doesn't make you a monster! As Kirsten McLean shows us in the following, we need to make sure that we are acknowledging and caring for young people's realities rather than trying to squeeze them into socially constructed categories.

Out of the shadows: talking bisexuality in the classroom
Kirsten McLean

Social and cultural notions of sexuality divide it into two mutually exclusive categories – homosexual and heterosexual. Within such a binary, there is no place for bisexuality. Therefore, those young people who identify their sexuality as bisexual are commonly understood to be confused, in denial of their true homosexuality, or psychologically maladjusted. Perhaps the most enduring impact of the binary, however, is to make bisexuality and bisexual people invisible. When this invisibility occurs in the classroom, the impacts on young bisexual people can be devastating.

Mr Lee coughs loudly to get the Social Science class to be quiet. 'Today,' he says, 'we will be discussing gay and lesbian issues as part of our current unit on sexuality.' Despite loud guffaws from the back of the class, he starts to read an article about what it's like to come out as a gay or lesbian teenager. Sal feels her palms begin to sweat, and her throat constrict ...

Kirsten McLean

Mr Lee has finished, and the class is busily discussing the issues.
Words clang in Sal's ears – gay, straight, lesbian, hetero …
Her head feels light, and she looks around at her classmates anxiously,
hoping no-one's noticed.
'What about me?' she thinks. 'Where are the words that describe
what I am?'

When young people are coming to terms with sexual attractions to both men and women, such invisibility creates a feeling that their sexuality is not genuine or real. The confusion this creates can have enormous impacts on self-esteem. Even when attempts are made to make the curriculum more inclusive of sexual diversity, simply referring to gay, lesbian and heterosexual lives reinforces the heterosexual/homosexual binary.

Sal shifts uncomfortably in her seat. The class is still discussing the
article about gay and lesbian teenagers. 'Why do we have to talk about
it?' she thinks. It's bad enough that it's all she's been thinking about
lately. Now this is reminding her of the choice she needs to make.
At first she thought it was just a phase. In Sex Ed they said it wasn't
unusual for teenagers to have crushes on people of the same sex, and
still turn out 'normal'. The problem now was that she couldn't shake
off the phase, no matter how hard she tried. But she couldn't have it
both ways, she knew that. What could she do?

Many young bisexual people are made to feel they must make a decision to be either straight or gay. The invisibility of bisexuality in mainstream understandings about sexuality, and its subsequent invisibility in schools, increases the likelihood that young people will hide their bisexuality from peers, friends, families and teachers. Many young bisexual people believe secrecy about their bisexuality is easier than attempting to explain it to others. This comes at the cost to their emotional, mental and spiritual health created by internalising feelings of isolation, hurt and despair.

Sal sits with her friends at lunch. Vicki's telling Lucy about the article
she read in a magazine about a pop star rumoured to be gay. 'He's gotta
be gay. He should just admit it.'

'But he's always got women in his videos,' Lucy argues. 'And he sings about liking girls. He's straight!'

Sal chews her food slowly to avoid entering the conversation.

'Naah, it's just a cover, he's sooo gay,' pipes in Chris.

'What do you reckon, Sal?' Lucy asks, wide eyed.

She avoids eye contact with them. How can she tell them? How can she even try to explain that it's not as easy as they think – that for some people the words gay and straight may not apply?

'Um … er, I dunno. I haven't really thought about it,' she lies.

In mainstream media, gay and lesbian characters are emerging in popular television programs but the same hasn't occurred for representations of bisexuality. Any visibility of bisexual people is more often than not based on false or misleading stereotypes. In particular, bisex-ual characters in films and television shows are often represented as evil, deceitful, confused, or sexually promiscuous. Such stereotyping not only presents a false picture of what bisexuality is, but also reinforces the invisibility of bisexuality by presenting it as an unacceptable identity option.

Mr Schmidt comes into the classroom, his face stern with anticipation. Today he has to teach a difficult topic, Sex Education, and it's the first time he's ever done it. But he wouldn't want his class to know that.

Mr Schmidt swallows slowly as he begins. 'OK, everyone, today we are going to discuss HIV/AIDS …' Before he can finish Vincent cuts him off.

'I was watching TV in the holidays, and they said that this doctor was sacked because he had sex with his patients and had AIDS.'

'It wasn't just that,' Amira yells out. 'He did it in his

surgery, and without his wife knowing. And with men and women.'

'Oooh, that's so disgusting,' her best friend Caroline adds. 'Those bisexuals just spread diseases around.'

The class descends into chaos as stereotypes and abuse fly around the room. Mr Schmidt just looks on, frozen with fear about how to deal with such fervent but misguided comments.

Sal sits at the back of the classroom saying nothing. She's furious, and struggles to hold back her tears of frustration. 'Why isn't he correcting them?' she thinks. 'I can't believe he's letting them say those things!'

Later, in the staff room, Mr Schmidt holds his head in his hands. He knows he should've handled that much better. But what could he do? 'Kids nowadays know far too much about sex,' he thinks. 'More than I do.'

Without positive role models, or with only inaccurate and often harsh representations of bisexuality, young people who are beginning to become aware of their bisexuality may mistakenly believe that to be bisexual they must conform to a particular set of stereotypes and behaviours that are represented in popular culture. This greatly affects not only the self-acceptance processes of young bisexual people but also increases the likelihood they will suffer from low self-esteem.

There are few resources available in schools for young bisexual people. Books in libraries, the availability of pamphlets from health and welfare staff or simply the recognition that bisexuality exists can mean the difference between developing a healthy sexual identity and continuing doubts and fears about one's sexuality created by secrecy and guilt.

The school curriculum needs to recognise that sexuality is better understood as a continuum on which there is a range of positions. It needs to recognise the diversity of sexualities rather than presenting heterosexuality as the only option, or presenting sexuality as a simple binary of heterosexual or homosexual. There are a number of strategies teachers and education professionals could implement to allow for the recognition of bisexuality as well as make the curriculum more inclusive of all sexualities:

▶▶ Examine the heterosexual bias within the classroom. For example, in the History curriculum, students could be made aware of the differing perspectives on the everyday lives of historical figures. Some accounts of the lives of Alexander the Great and Julius Caesar discuss their relationships with both men and women, yet this is rarely mentioned in classrooms; rather, the focus is on their heterosexual relationships. This technique erases bisexuality as a possible component of the lives of these important figures – and erases bisexuality as a legitimate sexual preference.

▶▶ Challenge the use of a heterosexual/homosexual dichotomy to represent the spectrum of human sexuality. Do discussions about 'alternative' sexualities mean 'gay and lesbian' sexualities in your classroom? Do you ever mention the word 'bisexual' – or acknowledge that some people do not want to label themselves at all? Do discussions about sexual diversity take place at all?

▶▶ Make the classroom more inclusive of bisexuality by working with representations that stereotype or erase bisexuality. As the media is a primary source of information through which students receive messages about sexuality, these sources can be used to examine and critique the ways the media presents us with a distorted view of the reality of sexual diversity. For example, show the students a range of representations of GLBT people and ask the students what's missing from these representations. This question invariably leads to a lively discussion, not only about the reasons for such imbalanced representations, but also the impacts of these representations on those who identify as GLBT.

An ex-colleague once said to me that 'these things' don't need to be taught in schools. To argue this point is to deny that our classrooms are made up of students with a wide variety of social and cultural identities, some of which will not be obvious to us. The task, then, is to find ways in which the experiences of all young people can be validated in the classroom, and to include positive and affirming representations of all sexualities.

'Does anyone know who Shakespeare addressed these sonnets to?' Ms Campbell asks. Sal knows that Shakespeare wrote some of the sonnets to a young man, but she remains silent.

No-one speaks, so Ms Campbell answers her own question. 'In the first 100 or so sonnets, Shakespeare addresses them to a young man. While Shakespeare was married, many people have speculated about what relationship Shakespeare had to this young man. Whether the relationship was a sexual one or not we don't know, but it certainly appears to be an intense relationship filled with great emotion and love.'

Faces in the classroom change as the students think about what they've been told, but no one reacts. Sal cannot believe her ears – did

Ms Campbell really just tell the class that Shakespeare possibly had both male and female lovers? Smiling to herself, she puts up her hand to offer the class some information she's read about who this young man may have been. As the class intently listens to her speak, she can't help thinking: 'At last!'

131

Sexual diversity and teachers

In the following two contributions, the importance of professional development for teachers is presented by two teacher trainees. Why do some people believe that being GLBT and being a teacher are mutually exclusive categories? What impact can homophobia have on teachers' wellbeing, and their ability to be effective educators and supportive of all students?

Jackie Ruddock gives us insights into the tensions that can occur in being a lesbian and training to be a teacher. Hilarie Zwaller then talks about the need for sexual diversity training for all teachers. In both personal reflections, the importance of teachers being trained in how to do 'inclusivity' is made very clear.

What's still hiding in the 'hidden curriculum' and the adventures of a young dyke

Jackie Ruddock

I'd like to introduce myself to you. Well, actually, I'd like to introduce us to you.

There's me – Jackie One – the graduated high school teacher, currently doing postgraduate research in education. She's the one who walked into the classroom on her first day of teaching to hear the students ask one another, 'Do ya reckon Ian Thorpe's gay?'

The other Jackie – Jackie Two – is the 23-year-old dyke whose heart skipped a beat as she thought, 'Oh god, imagine if they then ask me if I'm gay. And, what the hell do I think I'm doing becoming a teacher!' Of course these two Jackies are one and the same; but their reactions to the education system can be quite different. Let me explain.

As part of undertaking a degree in teacher training, university students are required to perform 'micro-teaching': an exercise in which fellow students pretend to be school-aged people, and we, acting as a teacher, give a fifteen-minute presentation. You'd be surprised at what you see:

A male stands in front of the class (fourth-year university students pretending to be thirteen-year-olds!), and tells them, 'Today we will be working on our family trees.' We're supplied with paper and pens. 'Now,' he says in a rather stern voice, 'please put the name of your father and mother at the top of the page, and I'm assuming you all have a mother and father.'

The mention of a family tree draws me – Jackie Two – back to my own student experiences in the Japanese language classroom, when I had to ask about how step-parents and de facto relationships 'fitted' into the branch framework. (Finding out what 'stepfather' was in Japanese seemed difficult enough among the 'normal' nuclear families. Maybe that's one reason why I stayed closeted at school!)

But it's also the word 'assume' that jolts and surprises me – Jackie One. Am I to be punished if I don't have 'a mother *and* father'?

After the pretend lesson is over the lecturer quickly – while constructively criticising the 'micro-teaching' – explains that perhaps the student teacher's language of assumption may not be so appropriate any more. Indeed. Here, the 'hidden curriculum' looms large. Many of the student teachers themselves questioned: What of the student without parents? Of only Grandma Pat? Or of parents Jill and Priya? Of Derek and Matthew? Of families divided by country entry and non-entry limitations? Of a family with the eldest brother as guardian? The 'family' has changed, and we learn – we are taught as teachers – to respect and allow for these realities in the school system.

But there is another example lesson in my university course that I wish to share. And this time, it's the lecturer who runs the practice lesson:

An exercise called 'My ideal date', in which the university students (once again pretending to be school-aged people) have to pair up, one person physically describing their 'ideal date', the other person drawing the descriptions. It's set up as a good communication task, a good 'getting to know each other' exercise.

Fine. The problem is I – Jackie Two – am paired with a girl I hardly know. And here I am wondering what will happen when I describe my 'ideal date' as an Angelina Jolie. Sure, I'm 23 years old and 'out' to most people around me, but it sure as hell doesn't stop my heart from racing. If I do this task 'properly' (read 'truthfully') the whole class is going to learn my sexual orientation. Do I want my peers knowing this? Do I want my lecturer to know this? The environment suddenly feels distinctly heterosexist.

So then, while Jackie Two is grappling with what she's going to do, Jackie One begins to question: Well, what of a twelve-year-old student that's been given this very same, and very common, task? What happens when her mind may be picturing a girl who sits next to her in Geography? And instead – because of her classmates' and her teacher's assumptions – she has to describe some boy 'ideal' because that is what the exercise is about. Do you know how that makes her feel? Well, it makes Jackie Two feel as though she's lying because the way I think is 'wrong'. And that brings with it an inherent 'I must be bad'.

Are we questioning all our teaching assumptions enough? Unconsciously, subconsciously – and, unfortunately, quite consciously – some teachers ignore the differing realities of their students. I realise the job is a difficult one – a huge undertaking. It's because I respect the profession that I write my experience. Nor do I want my sexuality (or anyone's) to dictate my life: but it does when you have to edit everything you're going to say (that 'hidden heterosexual curriculum').

That's why we are writing this: Jackie One, so that she can be an effective and proud teacher (who happens to be queer), and Jackie Two, the young dyke, who while negotiating her identity, is going to be here and queer.

> There are teachers who are gay and don't want to come out. I know one teacher like that and I told him some of us parents would support him. **A dad**

> A lot of the young teachers coming through won't have these homophobic attitudes. I do have faith in the younger ones. **Janine, a mum**

Knowing the 'plumbing' isn't enough
Hilarie Zwaller

Science teachers in schools may be called upon to teach sex education classes. In a seminar on sexuality education I attended, issues of power and gender were discussed, as was the subject of same-sex attraction in students. We were advised to explain to students that some people are heterosexual, bisexual or homosexual and this can be an evolving process, or people may take one path or another, sometimes for life, sometimes only for a certain time. However, during the course of the workshop, our leader advised us to be cautious about giving advice to students on the subject of homosexuality, as it was still a controversial issue, and that it's important to know the school's policy and to ensure that there's parental approval or at least to have approval from the school principal.

Oops! Too late for me. I'd already been on teaching rounds and had been presented with a question on that very subject and I *had* given advice. Fortunately, as part of my previous work history, I had been involved in instructing health professionals in safe-sex practices, as well as discussing with these students the best ways to broach sexuality issues with their patients. When the secondary school student asked me the question, I felt comfortable and felt I was able to assist her. How many other student teachers would have approached the situation in the same way as I had? How many would've been able to offer advice that put the student at ease? How many would've been embarrassed and brushed the student off?

How would experienced Science teachers deal with such questions? The student confided to me that she had asked her teacher and had been told that she was 'a horrible girl'. I knew that she was telling me the truth as my supervising teacher warned me that the student was 'a horrible girl' who 'asked such strange questions'. I would argue that the questions were not unusual given the circumstances; the student was in a relationship with another girl in the same class, I'd seen them kissing at a drama rehearsal when they thought no-one was looking. Imagine the courage that this student must have had to risk rejection for the second time!

This brief anecdote of mine raises the issue that the professional development of teachers in these areas is glaringly inadequate. This is particularly important for Science teachers, like myself. In junior science the male and female reproductive systems are usually covered, as is the biological basis of puberty. I'm also a Biology teacher, and human reproduction and development is studied in depth at senior level. Why is it that a teacher is expected to know the 'plumbing' without being required to have the skills and the ability to field questions from students that relate to sexuality and sexual desire? Isn't it reasonable to assume that students will want to know more than just the names of 'the bits'?

They're training up teachers now at unis to do sexual diversity education who then go into schools and come up against, dare I say, older principals and teachers saying 'Whatever you're learning at uni, you can't put it into practice here.' So they say, 'But we've been taught this skill, this policy, this curriculum package!' **Naomi**

Pooftas, pizzas and pedagogy
Daniel Witthaus

As a nineteen-year-old I was a project worker for a young GLBT support project. I would often feel helpless and frustrated as I put a bandaid on GLBT young people and sent them back into battle with a hopeful yet unsatisfactory, 'I hope you have a better week at school.'

In expressing my frustration to others, I would have many conversations with youth workers and teachers. Generally they were sympathetic to addressing homophobia within schools, yet tended to add, 'But you can't do that in schools, you just can't.'

Typically I struggle to accept 'no', 'can't' or 'won't' as an answer. I was determined to bash my head against this brick wall. I couldn't wait for top-down approaches so I decided to focus on what I could do. For twelve months I read and discussed as widely as I could, developing ideas and learning more about working within secondary schools. And soon, my program, 'Pride & Prejudice', was born.

Let me take you back to how it started.

Week One — Going in cold: I often describe working with the school prior to the students as the storm before the calm. It has been my experience that working with young people is the interesting, challenging, fun, exciting part. Working with staff at schools can often be hard going, due to:

▶▶ teacher perceptions about how young people will react – or over-react – to discussions around GLBT issues;

▶▶ the potential for negative reaction among the wider school community;

▶▶ homophobia within the institution as well as the staff;

▶▶ the lack of opportunities for complementary initiatives to an isolated yet effective program.

My first ever group of students was at an all-boys' Catholic school. This opportunity arrived after eighteen months of working with staff, working groups and key teachers in a series of meetings. Finally,

I was going into a school! And so commenced what would be eight weeks with the 25 students of 9JB.

My heart rate increased dramatically and I felt like I was faced with a sea of unwelcoming faces. Despite all the passion, motivation, excitement, preparation and opportunity, it all now boiled down to this moment of truth. I was a young gay man – incidentally an atheist – standing in a classroom complete with Jesus on a cross – at a Catholic all-boys' school about to begin a process that I had no certainty would work. Would I make a difference? Was God really real, and would he strike me down for this? Would they guess I was gay before the crucial fourth session? Why am I doing this? Why are they letting me do this?

I'm always nervous before working with a group, typically freaking and stressing out because this work is so important to me. I generally break all of the rules, speaking too quickly and forgetting to breathe. This occasion was no exception. My one saving grace was that at some point I forgot and everything began to flow as I got to the fun bit of me doing my thing up the front.

Daniel Witthaus in action

During the first session, 'Difference and our reactions', I concentrate on four things:

1.   exploring the concepts of difference and normality
2.   discussing mainstream social acceptability
3.   relating difference back to students and their context
4.   rapport building.

The last point is perhaps the most important. The young people need to get comfortable with me. This includes my customary clumsiness where in my excitement I accidentally trip over something in the room. This typically helps lighten the mood. No matter what, by the session's end, I attempt to know most of the names and personalities in the class, if for nothing else than the sake of class management!

From my diary: Before I knew it the bell had rung, with a subsequent mad dash for the door. I felt the group seemed to be switched on. I did receive feedback that although a great session, I should consider being stricter in my class management, and ask the boys to take out their pens and books earlier in the class.

Week Two — Slow going: 'Framing a-gender' focuses on three main areas:

1.   introducing concepts of sex and gender
2.   exploring stereotypes about males and females
3.   discussing the ways males and females interact with the same sex.

There was no doubt that the first five minutes of the second week were hard going. After the customary 'what am I doing here?', 'is this really worth it?' and 'I'm gonna die', the session flowed through to a discussion of the typical characteristics of a male, which began with 'a dick'.

The highlight of this session is typically around the ways in which females, and in this case especially males, interact with the same sex. Same-sex affection is justified – or not – in some extraordinary ways:

'Boys fight, girls hold hands, that's the way it is';

'It's okay if you are drunk', 'on a footy field', 'if no-one else is around'.

When I asked the young men if they were interested in discussing gay men and lesbians further the following week, they all agreed unanimously. Phew!

Week Three — Here's where it starts to get really interesting: 'Not every-one's straight' covers a number of things, including:

▸▸ homophobia

▸▸ brainstorming words and characteristics associated with gays, lesbians, bisexuals and heterosexuals

▸▸ questions for gay and lesbian people from students.

I suggested that I would conduct video interviews with real gay and lesbian people and show them in the next session. The young men were asked what they might ask gay and lesbian people if they had the opportunity.

From my diary: *Every pair of eyes lit up, with a smile or look of shock on every one of the faces. Other qualifiers would come: who will you ask; how do you know them? One boy even asked me in desperation not to talk to them, expressing concern for my wellbeing ('I don't want you to!'). One thing that this proved was that my sexuality was not going to be questioned – I thought it might have. The questions kept coming until the bell. Off they went. One student grabbed a Year 7 and said, 'He asked if you were gay, sir' ('let him go') before running off himself.*

One student stood beside me at the board after the others had left, and while I dusted the board asked, 'Well, are you gay?' I told him I would answer everything next week, and to think about why knowing the sexuality of others can seem important. He qualified as he left that he was 'straight'.

I was now under pressure to find a video camera to rent, and to find gay and lesbian people who would be willing to participate in a video interview. While many volunteer in conversation, it's surprising and frustrating how people suddenly back out or get busy on the shoot day. I actually do understand this, and I think it demonstrates how much people invest in the coming out process. In the end I did get the time and courage of four gay men on video, and two lesbians through writ-ten responses. At some stage along the way I had a brainwave to video myself, which seemed much less confronting than coming out live.

Week Four — 'Happy birthday to me, happy birthday to me': And so — it wasn't planned — on my twenty-second birthday I arrived ready to reveal the sexual orientation of five people, including myself, to the students of 9JB in 'All your questions answered?' My stomach was in knots. Basically, I was terrified. My one consolation was that my interview had been completed on video, and all I had to do was press 'Play'. I silently congratulated myself over and over again for this accidental stroke of genius.

As the young men entered, I became even more tense, given that there were three teachers present. I felt like I was suddenly deemed incapable of managing the process. My anxiety dropped when one young man asked 'Did you bring any gay people with ya?' I smiled, 'Yes, we're watching the video, remember?' and asked for everyone to be seated quickly. After reading out the written responses of the lesbians, I played the video that showed four brief interviews with four openly gay men.

Questions followed — 'How do you know them?', 'How did you meet them?'. When asked if it had been worthwhile to show the video, *yes* was the overwhelming response (a fact that *all* teachers need to know). When pressed, students remarked that they realised gays were real, and 'normal'. (One even remarked on his surprise that gays had jobs.) They told me that the people on the video were not what they'd anticipated.

I then told them I had one more person to show them on video, at which point the tension built as I went to press 'Play'.

The moment of truth had arrived.

My intention to watch their faces as they saw me coming out didn't eventuate. I couldn't bear to watch anything but the screen, trying not to gulp continuously, hoping to remain calm. I'm not certain I pulled it off. In reality some young men were generally surprised, others not, and others having a moment of insight with nods, or uh-huhs.

The bell rang towards the end of the video. Unplanned, I breathed a sigh of relief. However, the customary stampede out of the room I needed didn't happen. Instead, for the first time, the young men sat attentively, almost out of respect, waiting for what needed to occur next. I apologised for not having more time and offered that we could talk further the following week.

From my diary: The general mood of the room seemed positive and buoyant, which I regret not having longer to work with. One student came up and shook my hand on the way out, with another stopping to ask if he could help with any future videos that I made, as he was interested in camera work. I said that there might be an opportunity for the whole class to continue with a project and he quickly added that he had a girlfriend who would be happy to help out.

It was an exhilarating feeling afterwards, not only for the responses of the young men. It meant that the hardest bit was over, and that the process had some merit.

That afternoon I left with a headache, but I eagerly headed back to the office to read the worksheets. This included:

▸▸ things they didn't expect to hear – typically that GLBT people were studying or working, none chose their sexual orientation, they have straight friends, blue is a popular gay and lesbian colour!

▸▸ after seeing the video, they felt more informed, a positive change in perceptions of gay and lesbian people, including their appearance and mannerisms.

I developed a blinding migraine – my first ever! Happy Birthday!

Week Five – Daniel in the lion's den? I began the fifth session 'What's it got to do with me?' I decided I needed to be as relaxed as possible, knowing that because this was new they were likely to take their cues from me. The session goes through:

1. an informal question and answer section
2. statistics and research relating to same-sex attracted young people
3. famous gay, lesbian and bisexual people
4. homowork – what they could do, like research, interviews, examining their homophobic attitudes.

Sitting on a table up the front, dangling my legs, I asked if anyone had any comments – you could hear the crickets rubbing their legs together! I then asked if there were any questions, and the class slowly began to warm up – with their questions amounting to:

▶▶ origins of sexuality – e.g. when did I realise I was gay?

▶▶ coming out – e.g. how did my friends and family react to me coming out?

▶▶ homophobia – e.g. do people at work talk behind my back?

▶▶ topical – e.g. do you want kids and what if you ever did? my thoughts on 'curing' homosexuality; people 'turning gay' after marriage and kids; homosexuality as a phase.

To end I spoke about possible projects – or homowork – that they could do before they saw me next. When I brought up 'talking to five people about what you've learnt', it was evident that most of them had spoken to many of their friends already! A challenging idea was 'befriending a known target of homophobia'. One student asked 'What if you've been giving them heaps?' 'All the more reason to,' I replied, relating how it might make a difference in a person's life.

I was invited on behalf of the young men to stay an extra week, allowing an excursion prior to the last session.

Week Six – Hanging out, pigging out: I arrived a little earlier at the pizza restaurant than did the busload of students. The bus rolled up. Once seated everyone began their pizza 'all you can eat' meal. I would observe my reluctance to sit down, thinking the young men who sat next to me might have felt uncomfortable. They weren't, it was my paranoia again. (Interestingly, a previously challenging student sat next to me and we talked a few times, with him seeming totally comfortable to discuss his ethnicity and school raffle ticket prizes.)

I also had the chance to talk to the form teacher, the year level coordinator and a student teacher. The year level coordinator commented that he thought a large part of my success was the fact that I respected and listened to the young men – as well as having a laugh every now and then without overdoing it.

Along with the students, I headed for the ice-cream bar. Two students asked about the rainbow flag, given there was a definite rainbow picture theme going on in the restaurant. I explained about the rainbow flag, and one of the young men told me about a house he'd seen one on. The young men even questioned whether the restaurant was actually run by GLBT people.

Education through
respect and
relating

We had a few laughs about ice cream. I challenged one young man to see how much ice cream he could get in his bowl – it turned out heaps, with ice cream spilling everywhere. I was waiting to get in trouble from the teachers!

Then, out of nowhere, one young man – an outstanding contributor during the entire program – got up and said a few words, thanking me for what I had taught his class. The form teacher spoke as well. I felt very warm and fuzzy.

We then left. I followed the bus for a while with the boys waving and sticking their thumbs up (at least it wasn't their middle fingers).

Suddenly I realised I had impacted more than I could've anticipated. If only for a few weeks, I had made a difference. Driving back to work I was struck with the realisation that the next week would be it. All of a sudden I felt horribly sad.

Week Seven — Is this the end? Driving to the last session I wondered over and over if it had been worth it. Could I say the beautiful and meaningful things that would inspire them to continue thinking critically long after our sessions were over? Alas I knew that the 'damage had been done'. I knew they would've made up their minds by now if they were going to take everything on board, or to say, 'Yep – there's this faggot that stood up in front of us for seven weeks.' But what would they think? I knew that I had to be prepared.

'Bringing it all together' involved:

1.   revisiting homowork
2.   recollections/reflections by students
3.   community groups, information, etc.

I asked for an update on their 'homowork'. One student spoke about saying hello and talking to a teacher ('we think she's a lesbian'). Another young man told of how he and a friend had asked their graphics teacher if they could do something around gays, lesbians and homophobia. Fantastic! Others 'forgot'.

I asked for final comments or questions:

▶▶ Did I know the dux who came out two years ago?

▶▶ Do I know anyone at their school who is gay and if so how?

▶▶ How was the school I went to?

▶▶ How did people know I was gay in high school?

▶▶ Can I tell who is gay and who is not, more so than a straight person?

▶▶ Could the video be shown to all in their year level?

Then the bell went. I got a lot of goodbyes and even a cool handshake off one exuberant young man. And then it was over.

Part of me wanted to continue for a few weeks to capitalise on the more relaxed atmosphere. Another part of me wanted to collapse, emotionally drained from what had been a personal journey.

I had made an impact, and everyone appeared to have gained. Even some of the quieter young men offered that it had been important for them to just listen. The gamble had paid off – for me and the school – and I had become much more confident in the process.

Rather than celebrate, I got my customary donut and milkshake and wrote down my reflections on the experience.

The 'Pride & Prejudice' package was launched in early 2002. Pride & Prejudice is now being delivered in schools, both private and public, religious and not, single-sex and co-educational. For more details go to: www.prideandprejudice.com.au.

Coming out at a school is a huge step. It shouldn't be. It should be as easy as people knowing you're straight. Listen to some young people talking about their experiences of coming out at school.

Be prepared
The Pride and Diversity Youth Group with Shlom Eshel

Madison: When I came out at school, I was closer to a lot of my friends. For the teachers that wanted to know, there was no big issue. But my pastoral care worker – by the way, I went to an all-girls' Catholic school – she found it difficult giving me information regarding homosexuality, because she didn't know whether it was appropriate for her to be giving it to a young person.

John: Don't feel pressured to come out. I was pressured in some ways, but I ignored that pressure, and I did it in my own time. I felt like I needed to come out to the school. If they call you 'faggot' or a 'dyke', see it as a compliment because you're now open and you say, 'Well, I can accept that, what's the point of saying that? It's so old.' But you've got to do it at your own pace.

Madison: Be prepared. Be prepared for the mental, physical, emotional and psychological backlash that's going to come, because even if it may not be directly from a friend or a schoolmate, it is going to come and it's not going to make you feel too great.

John: And make sure that when you do come out, be careful who you tell. There are some very homophobic people who will go and bash people up. It's very twisted. Just be careful what steps you take and make sure you've got some support behind you, like youth workers or parents or someone. Don't do it by yourself, because I did that and it wasn't too good.

Josh: Instead of condemning someone and saying that you're going to go to hell, I think priests and religious schools should be accepting because hey, if we're God's creatures, then we're all equal and it makes

146

us no different. We're just labelled according to the society and it sucks. I spoke to the teachers at my school. They said that I was the only gay person at my school and yet I knew several other people who came up to me and said, 'I think I'm gay.' Younger people. If someone comes up to you, and you're a teacher, help them. Don't just push them away.

Madison: Educate yourself, teachers, before you say anything or do anything to a young GLBT person. Not just an understanding from a textbook's perspective but from a person's perspective. There are teachers who understand that they have a duty of care to all students. It's all students, despite race, disability, sexual preference, gender, whatever. If someone is being ostracised and harassed and bullied, teachers should do something about it. I don't want to be hearing that the teachers did nothing and just walked away, or they turned their back. It's not acceptable.

John: I left my school and went somewhere where you're looked after more.

Madison: You go through the process of finding out more about yourself and because of the stereotypes and people's bullshit being thrown at you, you start to believe them. But when you start learning about yourself, you realise, hey, that's not right.

In the following, Joel talks about how he used his schoolwork to help him come out. His teachers gave him opportunities to do research into sexual diversity. This is important for all students: to learn about sexual diversity and gender diversity across cultures, throughout history, as part of literature studies, as part of science studies, as part of civics and citizenship, legal studies, health education, community service, and the list goes on.

Ostracised by my peers but congratulated by my teachers
Joel Baker

When I was thirteen, I brought pornographic material to school in an effort to be seen as heterosexual and 'normal'. But it didn't work.

In the following years, I decided that it was time to let my feelings be known. I wrote research reports and feature articles on GLBT-related issues. For this I was ostracised by my peers but congratulated by my teachers. In one of my reports, my conclusion read:

'I am proud to be me, proud to homosexual. This doesn't mean that I am weird or that I am any different to the rest of my classmates. It simply means I am me, an individual ... '

In my last year of high school, more affirmed in my sexuality and willing to accept it for all the criticism it attracted, I've become a better person. I have found that I'm happier than ever. My friends are accepting and my family loves me.

In the following, Sebastian shows how schools need shaping up, not the GLBT student. He shows us the links between homophobia and sexism. Our school cultures need to turn their *hierarchies* of masculinities and femininities into the equal affirmation of the *diversity* of masculinities and femininities. If schools reward footballers as the best kind of boys with trophies, guernseys, airspace at assemblies and page-space in newsletters, are drama students, art students, musicians and dancers, and debating students, getting equal recognition and rewards?

The way the school responded to the bullying of Sebastian also illustrates how he was targeted further, even though he was the victim, rather than action being taken against the bullies. So what are appropriate teacher interventions and support? Certainly not methods that target and marginalise the GLBT student further.

Sebastian's story makes us face a tough question: to what extent do school culture, disciplinary measures and pastoral care interventions actually further bullying the bullied students? To what extent are they propping up and perpetuating a system that permits and rewards this bullying and hierarchy?

And, of course, how was Sebastian meant to actually learn anything while this was going on?

Sebastian worked very hard on himself, found support groups outside of school and on the Internet. He survived self-mutilation and suicide attempts. He stayed away from drugs. Some students don't get through like he did.

Is it the responsibility of the student to put up with all this as well as focus on learning and getting through adolescence? Sure, we want young people to be resilient, to be able to handle life's knocks. But, could the idea of 'developing emotional resilience' in young people be abused if it comes to mean that school systems and adults can abandon their responsibility for the safety and wellbeing of all students? Why should individual students 'toughen up' rather than adults think about the homophobic school culture they've put in place, which we expect young people to 'deal' with?

Once upon a time . . .

Sebastian

I've come a long way in the last six years. Looking over those years is extremely surreal. It feels like it was one of those extremely over-the-top soap operas.

When I was eight, my parents sent me to a Catholic school. A sports-mad, all-boys' Catholic school. How fitting for me to be sent there, especially since the word 'sport' is not actually one that is in my vocabulary. The other guys picked up on this and began imitating my speech and mannerisms. This was fantastic! New school, no friends, and I was the odd one out. Did I mention that I was a dancer? Great moment when they found that out. Fun!

Fast forward to my first year at high school. It wasn't all that bad actually. I had made quite a lot of friends, although I would receive the odd payout … 'fag', 'poof'. Being as naïve as I was, I had no idea what they meant and that I'd become well acquainted with the terms for the next five years.

Second year of high school came and stayed for an excruciating amount of time. No matter how hard I tried it wouldn't go any faster. As well as having to deal with unwanted body/facial hair, a voice going berserk and tweaking a not quite right image, I had to deal with other boys' insecurities. It's like they all knew something I didn't. Who would know the word 'fag' could hurt someone so much? It did. It led to numerous attempts to kill myself. My mates would ask me why I had bandaids on both wrists. I'd tell them that my cat went quite psychotic while I was washing it. Problem: I didn't have a cat and they knew it.

Each night in my room, I would tell myself, 'I'm not a fag. I don't like guys. I'm going to get married, have kids. I'm so very normal. So what if my best friends are girls, I love pop music, and I have every single record in the Spice Girls back catalogue (including all US, UK and Japanese releases)?' End of discussion … with myself.

The bashings started at the school cadet camp and continued on buses, at after-school hangout takeaway places, at school, everywhere. I didn't dare tell anyone. I was scared that an adult would think that I was a 'poof'. At camp one teacher knew that something was up because he found me under a bed crying. He didn't ask me what was wrong, just to clean myself up. I couldn't wait to get home. Not once did I ever fight back. I figured God wanted it this way for, if he didn't want it to occur, he would put a stop to it. I know better now.

One day at school I opened my locker to find a gay magazine and a wooden model of a mobile phone with the word 'fag' on the display. I threw up after fleeing to the park crying. When I decided to tell the year coordinator, he tried to make me see the humorous side of the episode. But what was so funny about what they did? They hated me so much that they went to the trouble to make a phone and buy a magazine. Definitely not funny. All this time I continued to blame myself.

I lost a lot of mates that year. A lot of them turned their backs on me as they were getting dissed also. Only two stood by me and I love them dearly. There were these three gay guys in a senior year. I became friends with them. We started to hang out a lot. It was fantastic! It felt so good knowing that I belonged somewhere. That sense of belonging meant the world to me.

They hung out away from all the playgrounds. They were afraid they'd get bashed or face further persecution. Afraid to be gawked at. Afraid.

At the end of the year, the graduating class threatened to pour tar and feathers on us. Somehow the deputy headmaster found out and placed us in the school office for a week or two until they had graduated. Airborne fruit and sandwiches became a daily ritual as did dodging them. It's not right – why were we seated in the office? We weren't hurting anybody.

One day in Computing Studies when I was fourteen, I walked to my seat and found 'Sebastian is a fag' on the computer screen. The same was on all the other computers. I left. I didn't go back to school that afternoon.

In Science, I'd have stationery and chairs thrown at me. We had a teacher who was having trouble with the class and couldn't control what they were doing to me. It was an extremely scary time. The sight of me running away from school wasn't an uncommon one.

Because of all this my school marks dropped and I became very defensive. At home my parents were on my back continually due to my performance (or lack of) at school. I'd get home from school, lock myself in my bedroom, and cry. I stopped eating, thinking that it would be a waste of food, that I wasn't worthy. Scared that my parents would find out, disown me and kick me out, I told them nothing about what was happening at school or in me. But I would dread going to school each day.

The Internet became an excellent outlet for me to chat to others about their experiences. It helped me so much. Surfing queer guys' sites and reading about how they dealt with bullying. A recurring theme was the need to build a network of gay and bisexual mates.

Last year, at fifteen, I went to a support group. They were all older than me but they were all going through this internal battle that needed to be calmed. We discussed safe sex, what it meant to be gay, our fears and thoughts on our situation. I became extremely comfortable with myself and my sexuality. I was gay and that was cool. The self-infliction of pain stopped.

My only problem now was at school. I came out to my best mates and they were fine. It was no shock to them. From then on, if anyone asked me if I was gay, I'd reply with things like, 'Take me out to dinner and you'll find out.' They were taken aback by my attitude. I didn't care any more what they thought. I took off my mask, I wasn't going to lie to myself any longer. I owed it to myself.

Now at school, younger guys have come out to me and expressed their fears and thoughts about their sexuality. I'm glad they feel comfortable enough to talk to me and that I'm there for them.

Through having a healthy attitude towards myself and being positive, people see that and admire me for it. Just last night my mates and I had a 'Queerfest'. They're all straight but we had a laugh and that's what it's all about. Like I said, I've come a long way. All my friends and a large majority of my grade and school staff know. My friends love and accept me and I feel like I belong. But best of all, I'm not afraid to go to school or be at home any more.

And I lived happily ever after …

I think I might be gay

Michael Crowhurst

How can a classroom teacher respond to a student telling them that they're gay?

GLBT students are unlike other groups of students who encounter discrimination in school settings in the sense that sexuality, unlike the colour of a person's skin, for example, is in many ways invisible. Because of this, GLBT students can sometimes escape direct harassment by passing as straight. Passing as straight can mean changing what you wear, changing what you say, changing how your voice sounds, or changing how you walk. It's perhaps not all that surprising therefore that most teachers have never encountered a GLBT student and are unsure about what to do if they do. In fact, when I was a high school teacher, only two students ever came out to me.

One student came out as bisexual during a legal studies class where we were discussing newspaper reports on lesbian access to IVF technology and how the law should respond to this issue. There were different points of view in the class and the discussion was fairly polarised. At one point a student said that she didn't think lesbians should have children and this is when another student, who I will call Peter, hurled the fact that he was bisexual into the discussion.

The class became silent. Initially I was unsure about whether this was a statement of truth or whether it was just a student 'mucking around'. My gut feeling was that he was telling the truth. He seemed nervous and self-conscious after making the statement. I was left speechless for a moment (which is very unusual for me). All that came to me to say was: 'That's okay.' I then moved the discussion on and refocused the class onto written work to reduce the tension.

After class I spoke to the student welfare coordinator and told him what had happened. I said I was concerned about Peter and about how the rest of the class would react, in the long term, to the news. He listened and said that he was unsure about what to do in this situation as this was the first time a student had come out in such a public fashion at the school.

The next day, Peter stayed away from school. The student welfare coordinator spoke to his homeroom teacher, who spoke to all of the other teachers who taught him. We decided that as Peter had made a public statement, and as this would most probably become public knowledge throughout the school, that it was acceptable to discuss this with other members of staff. Essentially teachers kept an eye out over the next couple of weeks in order to ensure that Peter didn't encounter any harassment. We discussed whether we should ring him at home to check that he was okay. We decided not to but in retrospect I think that it would've been prudent to do so.

Peter came to school the following day, looking tired and stressed out. He was withdrawn and seemed to be very self-conscious. He stayed behind the rest of the group at the end of the next legal studies class. I gave him a small postcard advertising a social support group for GLBT teenagers. He put it in his back pocket and moved towards the door. I said that if he wanted to talk to anyone he could ring them or he could speak to the student welfare coordinator or to myself or to anyone else on staff. I also made sure that he knew about the gay and lesbian switch-board, who offer a phone counselling service, and gave him the number.

He never spoke to me about his sexuality after that. I don't know whether he ever made it to the group or whether he spoke to other teachers. I decided that I'd leave it up to him to talk about these things if he wanted to and also not to put pressure on him to feel that he should go to a support group. He should only do what he was ready to do. He did seem less self-conscious as the weeks wore on, and the class didn't marginalise him in any way.

The other student, John, came out to me in a conversation. He was homeless and rarely attended school. We spoke for about an hour. He told me that he was 'out' at the refuge but that he didn't want to be 'out' at school. I told him about a support group and how to find use-ful phone numbers in the telephone directory. He listened to this and I had the feeling that he might attend the group I had suggested. In retrospect, I should've organised a taxi voucher or a lift for him to get there if he wanted that support. John didn't attend school for the remainder of the year.

I mentioned the conversation to the student welfare coordinator and stressed that I had reservations about discussing a private conversation. There's a tension here that needs to be discussed. It's very important to respect confidentiality but it's also important that conversations about sexuality are carried from private spaces into broader public arenas within schools. The next time a young person speaks to me about a sexuality issue, I'll explain to them why I think it's important that the broad details be discussed with the student welfare coordinator. I'd also explain to them that discussing broad details would mean that I might say something like: 'A student in Year 9 has come to me to discuss sexuality issues.' I would always seek to obtain the permission of the young person in this regard.

In light of the above experiences and my other work with young people, I'd like to offer a few brief points that might be some guide for teachers.

1. Listen to what the young person has to say with as little interruption as possible. Let the young person say all that they want to.

2. Recognise what a difficult thing it is to come out to a teacher and tell the young person this.

3. Reassure them that being GLBT is fine. If you are unable to do this you should seek counselling to deal with your own homophobia and refer the young person on.

4. After a while ask the young person if there are any issues at school that are causing them problems.

5. If the young person is being bullied, talk to them about this. Ask them what they'd like you to do about it.

6. Offer the young person counselling to deal with the effects of bullying but reassure them that they are not the person with the problem. Also ensure that the perpetrators of the bullying are required to undergo counselling.

7. Engage in dialogue with other staff to begin to unpack the structural features that might be generating bullying behaviours and attend to these.

8. If the young person is feeling isolated, it's imperative that you give them information about existing peer and other support groups.

9. As many young people won't ask a teacher about available supports, make this information available to students in the form of posters, pamphlets and student notices, and in school diaries and on school websites.

10. Ask the young person to come and see you again at a mutually convenient time. If you are aware of other GLBT young people, ask them if they'd like to meet others at their school and then find a way to make this happen.

11. Without (unnecessarily) breaching confidentiality, discuss this with colleagues and also how the school community might affirm sexual and gender diversity and minimise homophobic harassment.

Teachers need to arm themselves with education
YGLAM Youth Group

– What helps is having at least one teacher who's known as gay friendly. I had a teacher who had a Pride sticker on her car and in her office, and that was just a huge help. She'd instigate a lot of conversations with students about sexuality.

– I had one teacher who was completely open and strong and almost transformed the school in terms of prejudices. He still gets invited out to all the parties now. I think he was gay but couldn't come out to students. But occasionally he'd dress up as a traffic light or dress up in very full-on stuff, and always dye his hair a different colour until the principal said to get rid of it. People would be drawn to him and often we were learning with him to be exposed to different issues and think through our prejudices. It takes just one person in a school to be supportive and challenge and be there for you and you know you'll be okay.

– I would tell my teachers to talk about homosexuality because it was never talked about in our country school and everyone was so homophobic.

– I remember when I wrote a picture book about a gay couple. I read it to the class and opened it up for discussion. They didn't say a word. The teacher's comment on my book was about it being very interesting. Nothing to me about the issues or why it was important to me.

– There are some teachers who actively stop racism and racist comments, but within that same classroom you'll hear homophobic remarks that get left said. I think teachers need to arm themselves with education around what's acceptable.

Religious bigotry often poses as religious freedom in many of our private schools. These schools may be exempt from state laws regarding homophobic harassment and the inclusions of sexual diversity. As John Gascoigne writes in the following, the imposition of patriarchal moral absolutism in a school can lead to the justification and perpetuation of what could also be called 'immoral': the deliberate physical, emotional and mental harming of young people through discrimination, silencing and persecution. Another irony: in rigidly regulating a young person's religious beliefs, we are robbing the young person of developing a healthy connection between spirituality and sexuality.

The regulators

John Gascoigne

In *Les Miserables*, the policeman, Javert, is the enforcer, a man who simultaneously relies on an absolute and apparently divine moral code for his own identity and seeks to punish those whose actions contradict that moral code. When the object of his righteous wrath spares his life, Javert is unmanned, his absolute moral universe in disarray. In the stage musical, he sings about this on a bridge, moments before he leaps from the edge.

I also have stood in a high place, deliberating. This was because an absolute moral system, a Church of England high school education, specifically excluded me. I was and am gay. I was trapped – the Anglican God was the single path to salvation, but in His eyes my desires were sinful, an aberration. And even though I rejected the Anglican God, the disgust taught in his name for same-sex attraction was abiding.

A desperate choice that came close to fulfilment was one I made fully clothed, in a warm bath. I had labelled all my possessions for distribution. I held a hair dryer in my hand, switched it on and dropped it into the water. There was a moment of electricity: enough, I hoped, to shock me clear of the moral framework I had internalised, or at least my self-disgust. The lights dimmed, a bulb exploded, somewhere in the building a circuit breaker took effect, and I sat in darkness.

While my straight counterparts had female swimsuit models pasted proudly in the inside cover of their diaries, I prayed repeatedly to the Anglican God that my locker room fantasies be taken from me. I swore that I would never masturbate again, on pain of Hell, held out for two weeks, and felt a little more condemned each time I failed. I was simultaneously disconnected from my spirituality and my sexuality.

The Christian Studies department at my school was deeply conservative. In promoting abstinence, they attempted to discredit safe sex; we took notes from a video on the failure rates of condoms. Their condemnation of homosexuality was similarly unremitting. They referred to Romans 1:18–32, Leviticus 20:13 in the Bible, explained earnestly that it was a result of sin, a corruption of God's intention that sex be pri-marily for reproduction. They resorted even to crude arguments that bumholes were not made for penises, 'two keys and two locks', and horror stories about loosening sphincters and a need for adult under-garments in later life. They showed us a video address by a representative of the Exodus organisation. Exodus promotes the message of 'freedom from homosexuality through the power of Jesus Christ'. It attempts to 'cure' people of their homosexuality.

After seeing the Exodus video in Divinity class, another boy at my school came out to our school chaplain. He does not wish to be identified; I will refer to him as Tim. Tim was told by the chaplain that admitting his homosexual urges was the 'first step'. He was given a range of literature on the power of prayer in overcoming them, and was prayed for at lunchtime Crusader meetings. Tim was in Year 10 and by the end of semester he'd come to believe that: 'I was gay but I'm not now that God has helped me.'

The tone of the chaplain's response captures the paradox in religious pastoral care, which believes that it's acting in the best interests of students. In Tim's case, all the chaplain did was lay the groundwork for Tim's future mental illness.

The school's pastoral approach had a number of consequences. Tim and I were unable to form support networks with other same-sex attracted students, despite the fact that both of us had close friends who have come out since leaving school. Our internalisation of Biblical disgust led either to denial or frantic prayers. Although my friend and I had parallel experiences in school – he also considered suicide – we were unable to share those experiences.

The strategy I adopted at school was camouflage. One method was an emulation of heterosexuality. The fact that I had two girlfriends in Year 12 meant that I was beyond suspicion. Another, more hateful, method was the homophobic abuse of other students to distract attention from myself. I was called into my year master's office as a fifteen-year-old after my taunts reduced another boy to tears. I was asked why I had called him a poof, among other things. 'I think that he is, sir.' My behaviour was not punished. This sent a clear message about the school's tolerance of homophobia, despite the Christian directive to 'hate the sin, love the sinner'.

By the end of Year 11 Tim had decided that 'God doesn't fuck up' and to tentatively accept his sexuality. The following year he was 'outed' by a close friend at school. He spent that week 'curled up in bed with a knife ... the shame and embarrassment were unbearable'. Again, there was no official response from the school. This was another effective endorsement of homophobia.

Tim was hospitalised shortly before his exam trials. He had a 48-degree temperature and a massive swelling of the throat that threatened to block blood supply to the brain. The psychiatric team told him that the stress involved in being 'outed' was a major contributing factor in his illness. He never went back to school.

It is the right of the individual to determine a relationship – or not – with God, and to adopt a faith consistent with that relationship. My school and the Anglican diocese it represents failed to recognise this right. In the name of their particular faith, they became intent on imposing a moral framework on others. Any such viewpoint that attempts to limit God to one mode of access, or that excludes minorities from that access, should be resisted.

The freedom to practise religion must not be prioritised above a school's duty of care to its students. A 'moral' approach to pastoral care has to be reconsidered where it has a clearly demonstrated ill-effect on the mental health and wellbeing of students. The exemptions accorded to religious institutions and private schools in much anti-discrimination legislation should be reconsidered to protect GLBT youth.

'Merman' is a lullaby written for a gay man; it promises a dream life free of religious condemnation. 'The priests are dead,' sings Tori Amos, and the Merman does not need their permission to undertake his pilgrimage. It expresses a love for self that includes a love of sexuality. Too often, the self-esteem of GLBT people is constructed only with difficulty, in spite of the regulators.

I remember going down to my daughter's school, a school run by an order of nuns. I thought, 'Well, here we are, we're going to have to come out,' so I had a photo of my daughter and her girlfriend. I went up to the nuns and showed them the photo and talked about the girls, and they said, 'Oh, yes, we have to look after our gay girls.' And so I thought, 'Well, if they can be like so understanding, what are the bishops and priests going on about?' *Gillian*

Providing social groups for GLBT kids

Some young GLBT people don't feel they need support. They may have loving family. They may have lots of straight friends. But what they're looking to do is what most adolescents want – to meet and hang out with young people just like them, meet people they can have crushes on and go out with, look for potential intimate partners. How do we provide social groups for young GLBT people in our schools?

Searching for something a bit more social
Hayley

For the first couple of high school years I tried to conform and do all the things a good hetero should do, but by the middle of the third year I was fed up. So I stopped pretending and started to be gay Hayley.

My school liked to make a point of letting me know that they didn't like the new me. I got my eyebrow pierced – they told me to put a bandaid over it. I got purple bandaids – they told me to take them off. They even had the nerve to take me out of class and say in the nicest possible way that I had to grow my hair and stop wearing my Doc Marten boots because I was looking like a dyke – I left. I went to live with my aunty and her girlfriend for six months in another state just to get away.

When I came back the school was a little more considerate and I was less provocative. I thought that finding some gay friends was in order so I set out to find what groups existed. I found scores of support groups but I felt that I didn't need much more support than what my family was already offering. So I went out searching again, but this time for something a bit more social. What I came across next was an under-age dance club geared for the young GLBT community (Minus 18, coordinated and organised by PFLAG). As I didn't know anyone who would go with me, I was a little hesitant, but I decided that going alone and maybe finding some new friends was better than feeling alone.

At the Minus 18 event I saw someone that I recognised from school. It was bizarre that up until that point I'd thought of myself as the entire gay population of my school. After that I started to wonder who else felt the same. I started thinking how much I would have appreciated knowing there were more lesbians at school before then. Then I seriously thought about setting up a group at school in school time. The main problem I was faced with was approaching people about the group while still protecting myself against further harassment. I knew that at least one of the school counsellors, Jason, would help me so I proposed my idea to him. He thought it was a great idea and said he'd approach a few people he knew. Now the problem was the school itself. I knew that there was no way that this group would be able to proceed if the coordinators knew about it. But luckily Jason said he was prepared to keep it under wraps and lie for us.

The group met once but that was all. Jason seemed to lose interest or perhaps he was just too busy. At the time I thought he owed us a little more than the one token meeting, but by the small act of just allowing us to meet in school time Jason could've lost his job, a ridiculous prospect. I remember one teacher who I knew was gay herself just stood there and let a student scream obscenities across the yard.

It horrifies me to think that people are in a position to help and simply don't. Or are made to feel they can't …

Hi! Remember me?

Jen Blyth

If you're like me (old and decrepit at 24) high school might seem like a very long time ago. For some of us GLBT young people, the things that happened at high school mightn't affect us on an everyday level, but others might still feel the repercussions of the stifling existence that was secondary school.

Even if you've been out of school for a while, it doesn't mean that your experience at the school wasn't valid, and wouldn't have any significance for students and staff that are still there. No matter what your experience – good, bad or a bit of both – you as a former student have a perspective that schools may find invaluable.

So, what to do? How about getting back in touch with your old school? One way of doing this is writing an open letter to your old school, or a series of letters to various teachers in the school. You could tell them about your experience of being a GLBT student when you were there. What was good, what was bad, and what helped you. You have the power to help your former school gain an understanding of the issues that same-sex attracted young people might be facing, and what the school can do to ensure a safe environment for all students.

Here's an example of a letter you could send to your school – feel free to use any or all of this letter or modify it to suit what you want to write.

When you write your letter, it's important to keep it assertive, but not aggressive. This way it's more likely that what you have to say will be listened to and taken seriously, and you won't run the risk of your letter being seen as a threat and illegal.

Proforma letter: To Whom It May Concern

My name is <your name>, and I attended <school name> from <start year> to <end year>. When I was in <year level>, I realised that I was attracted to people of the same sex, and I am writing to you now to give you an indication of my experiences as a <gay/lesbian/bisexual/transgender> student at your school, in the hope that you will keep this in mind in relation to students currently enrolled at your school who may be same-sex attracted.

I didn't feel safe enough to come out at school, the homophobia I witnessed from the school yard and the classroom was more than enough to deter me from disclosing to anyone (including the school welfare coordinator) that I thought I might be gay. I was afraid that by telling people, I might become a target for both students and teachers, as other students at the school who were perceived to be gay were constantly the target of abuse, often under the witness of teachers. 'Faggot', 'dyke' and 'gay' were common insults in the courtyard that teachers often turned a blind eye to, convincing me further that to be gay is to be the worst thing in the world, and at times, it would be better to be dead.

Since leaving school, I have achieved a great many things, <provide some examples here>. One of the biggest realisations was that being gay is just another part of who I am, something that is natural, and something that I'm proud of. It took a great deal of time to achieve this realisation, and not something that I can give credit to the school for. My hope is that the students currently enrolled at your school can one day give credit to <school name> for helping them in discovering who they are, whatever that may be.

I believe that there are actions that may have helped me when I was at school, to facilitate my inclusion as a student who happened to be gay. <Provide examples of what you would've liked the school to do.>

I hope that I have provided an insight into something that you may not have been aware of, and that you now have the power to address. Thank you for taking the time to read this letter.

Yours sincerely

Part 3:

When our children come out in communities

What is community? What's it like *being* part of a community and yet *not part* of it, because there are aspects of you that your community does not accept? Each community has a set of codes and criteria for belonging. So in coming out, GLBT young people, and their families and friends, also have to negotiate 'coming in' to their various communities.

In this section, we're going to look at what we can do for GLBT young people in different types of communities such as rural communities, religious communities, ethnic communities, gay communities, workplace communities and communities of friends.

To begin, Peta Cox challenges us with why a simple gesture of love and affection like holding hands with her girlfriend while walking along a street of her local community is considered so scandalous.

Walking

Peta Cox

Walking down the street
People staring
Once again, as they have done before;
You'd think that love was a smiling matter,
A celebration even;
Obviously not –
They stare, and they scorn

It ends up that
Holding hands
Becomes the mortal sin
Of a generation,
Which is a horrid
Escape for the hate
All communities
Through all history
Have for someone –
anyone they choose
No logic –
just a scapegoat for all their sorrow

So,
I'm an excuse
For hatred
And I still insist
I love whom I do
Because love is worth more
Than hate ever will
And frankly to those who glare
I say: 'fuck you'

Daughter: Unless more and more people are understanding, it won't get any easier to walk down the street holding hands.

Parent: A couple of generations from now you'll be right.

Daughter: I can't wait that long.

Parent: I'll try to do what I can, my little bit.

'Our children are not offensive to the community'

My mother's far more out than I am in our local community but that's Mum's calling in her journey with my sexuality. She had no one to turn to and no resources out there and I think this is what gave Mum strength to say, 'I don't want that to happen to anyone else in our community.' I'm very proud of what Mum does. **Jo**

I've found that at times I've made angry statements to people and then I've said, 'Well, no, they're only coming from a place of fear and ignorance and I was there myself before.' So instead of jumping down their throat, I'll just try and talk to them about it. **A dad**

I wear my little rainbow badge everywhere. I was in the local supermarket one day when this woman came up to me and said, 'Oh, isn't your badge pretty. I've got one the same. It's pink. I support the women's breast cancer aware- ness. Where did yours come from?' I said, 'Oh, I support the gay movement.' Dead silence, and she walked away. **Bernadette**

Making local communities safe
Agnes Lichtor

Many GLBT young people fear venturing out alone in their local communities. Their trust in police and other authority figures can be shaky at best. Education for police officers is needed and identification and disciplining of homophobic police officers is important in order for re-education to take place.

Queer-friendly and accessible spaces are needed in local areas. Community-based support groups need to provide a safe, healthy atmosphere in which GLBT young people feel comfortable to disclose, seek support and break down the social isolation they may be feeling.

Support groups for friends and families in local communities are also important in order for families and friends to deal with their own underlying reservation about their loved one's sexuality, as well as offering support when situations are difficult.

Existing community health services and community centres that cater for GLBT young people and their families need to be publicised and promoted, as many are still inaccessible to rural and non-disclosed GLBT young people. Others simply are not aware of these services until they network with other GLBT young people, which is a challenge in itself. GLBT publications such as magazines and newsletters that advertise local events also need to be accessible as well as available. Local bookshops, community centres, cafes and libraries can carry information, magazines and books. They can also host guest speakers and other community events focusing on GLBT issues.

'Invisibility' in the local community is also a major issue, with many GLBT young people preferring to remain safely tucked away rather than face the threat of being attacked. Invisibility also refers to the community

opinion that GLBT young people need to remain in hiding. To target this, displays of art by GLBT young people, publication of GLBT young people's writing, educational talks, theatrical performances and other kinds of presentations in local community spaces will assist in flooding the community with information directly discrediting existing prejudicial opinions.

More education in various aspects of health and culture are also needed in local health clinics, such as GLBT-related information on sexual relations (the ABCs on 'how to do *it!*'), information on drugs and their effects, as well as support for those young people who are engaged in substance abuse. With these building blocks and baby steps, changes in negative community attitudes can be made.

Outing in scouting

Bryan

I started as a cub in scouting when I was nine. My father introduced me, as he was a leader, and I went through all the sections of my local scout movement. At age eighteen I decided that I enjoyed it so much I wanted to become a leader. I had good support from some adults I was working with who asked me to become a leader.

Earlier, I'd made a conscious decision when I came out to myself and to my family that I would stop being a leader because there was a lot of potential for messy situations being gay and being a leader within the local scouting community. That disappointed me because I really wanted to still be a leader. I could see how well I worked with younger age groups and provided development for people's children.

A very good friend of mine, who was a scout leader in our scout group at the time, and who had also grown up with me through scouting, asked me, 'Don't you ever miss being a leader?' This was after he found out that I was gay. I said, 'Well, yeah, but you can probably understand why I left and how difficult it could be.' He then said, 'You shouldn't feel that way. If you ever wanted to come back into the scouting community, I'd be more than happy to have you as one of my leaders. I've worked with you a long time and I really don't think you'll have a problem. But if you do, I'll be one of the first to defend you for what you've achieved through scouting and what you've provided for the community.'

That was a big plus for me, that was a big buzz – that I could challenge the community and still provide for people's children.

I'm still a leader. It's very empowering. I've just been myself, and developed a very close rapport with a lot of the adults, other leaders, the group leader, district personnel and committee people. At a district personnel meeting, one of the district leaders brought the paedophilia issue up. He said, 'Paedophiles like boys. Gays like men.' I actually had a birthday party last year, which was a gathering of all of the people I know, work friends, family, scouting friends, gay friends, and I am who I am with all of them.

What's offensive – nudity or gay nudity?

Community complaints about any event, festival or parade that is GLBT-focused – particularly if there is some nudity or risqué costuming – are all too common.

Challenge those complaints by telling people that GLBT culture is part of multiculturalism in the wider community and therefore the GLBT community is able to have its own cultural events.

Ask people if they're being consistent in their views about nudity in local community events. For example, would they say that the Venice Carnevale, or the New Orleans Mardi Gras, or those colourful festivals in Rio De Janeiro, where 90 percent of people have little on, are offensive? Or are predominantly straight parades and festivals okay, and their nudity and scant costuming 'artistic' rather than offensive? People either don't like these displays of nudity overall, or they are homophobic if they're selective about which ones are okay and which ones are offensive.

This year, my husband decided to march for the first time in the Sydney Mardi Gras. So last Monday night at his Rotary club, where he's the incoming president, he asked the current president if he'd be able to make a small, personal announcement. He got up and said, 'Well, I've got a suggestion for how to raise some money for the club. Some of you know that two of my three children are gay. I just wanted to let you know that this year, for the first time, I'll be marching in the Mardi Gras, with PFLAG, which is a parents' group, just to show my love and support for them. If any of you who are watching the Parade can tell me exactly what I'm wearing, there'll be $100 for the Rotary fund-raising.'

So not only was he very courageous to actually come out and say that to a relatively conservative club, but this also ensured that they all watched it and got the idea that the parade highlights serious as well as frivolous issues.

*He got very good responses and he thought the money was worth it. They cheered him, and a lot of people came up to him after the meeting. **Gillian***

Gillian Maury (3rd from l.)
and family at the Mardi Gras

Get heard on your local community radio stations, in local newspapers, at local public meetings. Contact community organisations, write letters, make calls, that either applaud any anti-homophobic work, or object to homophobic content and silences.

A letter to my local radio station
Maria F

First, I want to congratulate you on all the wonderful things you do for people who are in need of assistance in our community. It's very humbling to hear of all the people less fortunate who require our help, and it's great when your radio station goes to great lengths to help where they can.

Second, I want to voice my concern and disappointment at some of the remarks made on radio to a large audience, many of whom hang on every word.

This morning, I too, like the rest of your listeners in this community, was shocked to hear of the young boy who committed suicide at a local high school. It saddened me to think this young adult felt so desperate that he felt his only way out was to end his life. It was a nice gesture on the part of your radio station to convey condolences on behalf of our community.

However, in the next breath, a comment was made by the DJ about an article in the paper selling men's lingerie. The comments were to the effect that men wearing such clothing must surely be 'soft', 'pansies'.

I ask you, how do you know that that young man who committed suicide didn't commit such an act because of this kind of homophobic attitude endorsed by your radio station?

I don't know why this boy ended his life but surely there are enough pressures on young people these days about image, about sexuality, about 'fitting in' and being 'normal', about being successful at school, that they don't need such homophobic biases blared out from a supposedly reputable and progressive radio station?

Surely, being in the public domain, your commentators should take more care to consider that a huge range of people listens to your programs and that you have a responsibility to your listening public to be open-minded, non-discriminatory, tolerant.

My son, a sensitive eleven-year-old, has been the butt of much taunting by his peers because he's smaller, because he's sensitive and doesn't go around punching other boys to be 'macho'. He's called 'faggot', 'pansy', 'poofter', 'gay' constantly, to the point where we've had numerous meetings with the school staff to discuss strategies to deal with the problems. Yet, it's not my son who has the problem. It's the boys who think it's okay to bully and label in this way, who think that it's okay to harass someone who isn't 'tough enough', who might be 'gay'.

These boys, including my son, all listen to your radio station and look up to the DJ. His children attend the same school as my children and to these boys he's a cult figure. That's okay, but it's not okay for them to believe some of the homophobic stuff that's being conveyed on your radio station.

As a mother, as an educated person, as a former teacher and a person who believes in equality and acceptance, I strongly object to the discriminatory remarks made on public radio and feel that your radio station needs to address this problem and its responsibility to the listening public, especially to all the young children and young adults who tune in.

177

I was the community lesbian youth worker, an expert on sexuality

Caz McLean

A couple of years ago I started work as a youth worker at a local government authority.

On my first day the usual banter could be heard. Was I an asset or a dead weight? The usual anticipation surrounding any new employee. And then, before I knew it, the question was asked: 'Are you married?'

Without a moment's hesitation I replied, as any self-respecting lesbian would, that I was gay.

The words were well and truly uttered before I noticed various jaws either hitting the floor or clamping shut, as that familiar look of anxiety appeared that said so much without saying anything at all. But they managed an acceptable: 'As long as you're happy.'

It was then it dawned on me. I realised that I may in fact be the first living lesbian this parochial group had ever consciously laid eyes on. Now, instead of heeding the signs and retreating with dignity, I felt that overwhelming urge to compensate for their awkwardness by justifying myself. 'Yes, I am actually. Moving in with my partner soon. Totally in love. Never known happiness like it.'

Agh! I was appalled at my inability to shut up. It's your first day, I said to myself, they couldn't care less about you and your so-called 'alternative' lifestyle. Or worse still, maybe they do and you are now stained with the taint of 'sole lesbian worker'.

What happened next all unfolded in slow motion. I remember her walking towards me, golden halo intact, quite possibly an illusion that's developed over time, smile spreading generously across her face. 'Hey sister,' she said.

Little did she know these were the only words able to save me from the hole that threatened to swallow me so completely, the only words able to pry the foot from my mouth.

All eyes turned to the girl with the golden halo. It was clear from the look on their faces that no-one knew her secret, but now was suddenly the 'right' time for her to come out. Safety in numbers I guess.

It was only a couple of days later that a co-worker, let's call her Sally, approached me with a matter she wanted to discuss. Sally was a youth activity worker who had a young girl, let's call her Fiona, who wanted to discuss her sexuality. 'I'm only asking because you'd know what she's going through. I thought it'd be good if you talked to her. I haven't mentioned it to her. Wanted to ask you first.'

So there it was. In that moment I was no longer just another youth worker. I was the *lesbian* youth worker. Not that I minded. I didn't. It's just that I'd never thought of myself as much of an expert on sexuality. But there was no doubt it was me who was expected to support young people with questions about their sexuality. 'No problem. I'd be happy to talk to her.'

And that was the beginning. When Fiona came to see me, it was important that she feel safe and secure so I ushered her into the usually-avoided counselling room where we were assured, if not of atmosphere, then at least of privacy. Like most young people daring to articulate their fears and doubts to another for the first time, Fiona was very apprehensive. To alleviate her anxiety I made sure I mirrored her language. Labelling or referring specifically to Fiona's sexuality before she was ready would scare her away.

We spent around an hour and a half together that first time. I made sure she had as much time as she needed to say all she wanted. Fiona was eager to give me a picture of herself and quickly emptied her backpack onto the floor. With painstaking detail she explained the meaning of its contents: cigarette packets, empty drink cans, wrappers, train tickets. She told me about her best friend and the boyfriend she was with. She read me letters and poems, showed me schoolwork, talked to me about her family and school and the subjects she liked, teachers, talked about anything other than her sexuality. An hour passed. I waited. I watched as she slumped protectively over her bag, her eyes downcast. This was my cue.

'Is there anything you want to ask me?'

'It's weird.'

'What is?'

'You know, two girls.' She squashed an embarrassed laugh under her breath, careful not to look at me.

'What makes it so weird?'

'It's not natural.'

'Well, I was born this way so it seems pretty natural to me.'

'I don't care, it doesn't seem natural.'

'Who says it's not natural?'

'Everyone. Kids at school. Mum.'

'What's your mum say about it?'

'That all faggots should be shot.'

'What do you think about that?'

'I don't know.'

Every time a young person came out with stuff like this it took my breath away. 'Sometimes people say things without really thinking about them, Fiona. It's just something to say.'

'But my mum really means it.'

'Ok. She might mean it, but that doesn't mean she's right. Maybe she doesn't really understand what it means to be gay.'

'Mmm … '

I also assumed that if Fiona's mum didn't understand what it meant to be gay then chances were Fiona didn't understand what it meant to be gay either. 'Some people don't understand that if a person is bisexual or straight or gay then that's just the way they are. Sometimes if people, like your mum, don't understand, they can say stupid things. I couldn't choose to have a different body or a different head any more than I could choose to be gay or straight. No-one thinks redheads are abnormal and there aren't too many of them around, are there?'

'But how did you know?'

Now we were getting somewhere.

'Just a feeling inside, like I was different. I could never explain it and then one day it hit me. I knew I was a lesbian. After that everything just fell into place.'

Our conversation continued like this until we'd exhausted ourselves. After that Fiona either rang me or came to see me about twice a week for the next month. She continued to be negative for all of that time. Like many young people, Fiona had her own internal homophobia to deal with, perhaps one of the biggest obstacles to overcome, but I believe that meeting an adult lesbian who was alive and well was a start.

The next big step for Fiona was attending a support group for GLBT young people. After a lot of coaxing, cajoling and countless numbers of encouraging phone calls, Fiona arrived at her first meeting. While counselling and one on one with a worker is useful, there's no doubt that the only way to counteract the intense feelings of difference, isolation and loneliness experienced by those questioning their sexuality is by providing a safe, confidential space for young people to meet with others like themselves.

Over the next three months Fiona started her first same-sex relationship, came out to her best friend, and for the first time approached life with a growing sense of identity and self. The shroud of darkness that had characterised her life was lifting. While Fiona was still self-harming, this began to lessen. The writing she brought to our meetings was changing too.

Watching her open, beaming face as we marched down a main street with the banner we'd made especially for the Pride March, or hearing her words the first time we took a bus to the Minus 18 GLBT dance, when she rushed towards me saying, 'I never knew there could be this many gay people in one place,' are defining moments in my working life.

A year later Fiona attended the support group every week. No longer fearful of schoolyard taunts, she had the security of peers who could support her through the plethora of concerns she'd never dream of raising with me and finally believed there was no tattoo with the word 'lesbian' imprinted on her forehead. She was a young woman now, able to experience the growing up process, the right of every adolescent, a right that had eluded her in the past.

So what can a community group for GLBT young people provide? Throughout this book, you've been reading the comments and reflections from young people who are part of the Young Gay and Lesbian Group at Moreland Performing Arts Project (YGLAM) coordinated by Vicky Guglielmo and Jemma Mead. Let's see what young people say about why they joined this group and what it's providing for them.

You're not the odd one out
YGLAM Youth Group

- You get some confidence and support.

- I'd always wanted to make new friends and be with other young gay people.

- I think it's a space where you can feel the majority rather than the minority, you're not feeling you're the odd one out. People go out of their way to make you feel good about yourself. You meet young people who've been in a similar situation.

- In our group, we do theatre performance. This is a less intense way of expressing yourself than the one-on-one talk about these issues.

- It's a little bit freer when you're in a group because you share ideas and try things and you can be creative about what you want to express. It's a group where you can have whatever participation you need or want. And also it's run informally, that's important. It's friendly, there's no pressure, and you share experiences in that environment as well.

- You're not forced to be stereotypical or hide stuff about yourself. You can be more open without anyone getting you.

- I think a lot of the painful experiences and negative things that have happened in our lives, we can turn them into their opposite by being creative. You can turn them into something quite positive and beautiful. And I suppose, as an actor, you can actually be who you want to be here and know others are not going to put you down.

– We put shows on for the community, feeling like they can actually get stories, messages across, so we do some community education. So, what happens in here is most of the work is supporting us but it's also actually reaching out and sharing with the community, which will hopefully make things easier for other young people.

– For some young people who see our performances, it's almost their first exposure to anything about being same-sex attracted.

– When I perform, I might go bright red and shaky but I'm just trying to make the audience aware that the homophobic words that were coming out of their mouths weren't necessarily the right or positive thing to say to someone that's twelve or thirteen.

– I think this group provides you with skills, particularly how to deal with homophobic abuse. It makes me very well spoken. Lately I've been running into some kids in my neighbourhood who've been saying 'faggot' and 'poofter' and I'm like, 'Do you actually know what faggot means?' I also talk about what happened in the Holocaust or concentration camps and they're like, 'Oh.' So I'm learning skills and information that help me to teach younger kids to not say or feel homophobic things.

Photo courtesy of
Dianne Jeffrey

That's what (straight) friends are for

Straight friends have a very important role to play in the lives of GLBT young people. They can be allies, mediators and advocates. They can provide support and act as buffer zones against any homophobia being hurled at their GLBT friends. They can speak out against homophobia and not risk the same amount of bullying and harassment that their GLBT friends might face.

Generation Q

Mic Emslie

If a friend of yours
Says to you
That they are,
Or might be,
Lesbian, gay
Bisexual or
Transgender, then …

DON'T

don't be scared
don't run away
don't turn your back on them
don't judge them
don't go and tell other people without their permission

DO

do listen to them
do be there to talk to them
do be considerate
do be supportive
do be trustworthy
do accept them as your friend for who they are

SAY TO YOUR FRIEND

say to them that you will not tell anyone if they don't want you to
say to them that they are still your friend
say to them that they are the same person that you knew before

SUGGEST TO YOUR FRIEND

Suggest they might like to ring Lifeline, Kids Helpline, Gay and Lesbian Switchboard
Suggest they might like to talk to your student welfare coordinator at your school
Suggest they might like to talk to your local youth worker
Suggest that if you think and your friend thinks it's safe, to talk to your parents.

If you or your friend feel that a particular person is not the right person to talk to about how your friend is feeling then it is probably best not to talk to them. Find someone who it will be safe to talk to, who will understand your feelings and not judge you.

I go away annually on fishing weekends with between eight and fifteen guys. They're a whole lot of straight guys and I'm gay. If you can imagine a group of ten straight guys on a weekend away, there's always the 'Oh, gee, wouldn't it be good to have a girl here.' The first year that this came up, I just thought, 'I'm not putting up with this rubbish,' and I said, 'And her brother.' So every time we go away now, all the guys who've been going on this fishing weekend for years will say, 'Gee, wouldn't it be great to get some girls and their brothers on the fishing weekend next year.' **Paul**

Photo courtesy of
Dianne Jeffrey

Being out in the workplace community
Agnes Lichtor

For many young people, having a casual or part-time job means independence and a sense of self-worth. Being financially independent can boost a young person's self-esteem and self-satisfaction. While at work, feeling safe and non-threatened is the right of all employees, a right enforced by legislation. Unfortunately, many GLBT young people do not feel safe nor comfortable at work, regardless of whether they're 'out' or not.

Safety and a non-threatening environment can be compromised in many ways, some covertly, others more blatantly. Spreading rumours and gossiping are two potentially harmful forms of harassment. Because often it's done so covertly, the GLBT young person has little opportunity to challenge this harassment face to face. Often the GLBT young person isn't even sure who exactly in the workplace initiated the rumours or who's spreading them.

Veronica experienced first hand the damage rumours and gossip can create. 'I was working with my girlfriend at a fast-food place. At first the rumours weren't so bad. Then everyone got involved and the whole store, as well as employees at other stores, were talking about us.'

In Veronica's instance, the gossip and malicious rumours didn't stop at fellow employees; managers also contributed. 'It got really bad. Everyone would be talking about us, but no-one actually had the guts to come up to us and ask whether we were gay, whether we were really going out together. If they came up to me and wanted to talk about it, fine, I would've talked about it. I could've turned around and said, "Yeah, I'm gay, so shut up about it."'

Veronica was in a higher position in the company than her partner, and co-workers began to complain about their being allowed to work together. The situation escalated. The pressure was on them to be better workers than normal.

Eventually, Veronica and her partner took their case to the union, who acted as an advocate for them. 'We had a whole list of things we wanted to achieve. We did end up getting the company to implement, for the first time ever, a training program against harassment and discrimination. But it was only run with the people that were there already. They also did change the anti-discrimination part in the hand-book. Before, it used to be just a couple of lines long, now it actually went into a bit more detail.' However, not all the goals the girls set out to achieve were met. 'Our biggest point was to get apologies from the managers who were involved for not doing anything earlier. They never did apologise. I was told by the store manager that it wasn't his fault. He didn't see the harassment as a homophobic issue, he saw just gossip as the problem.'

Con's experience with workplace prejudice was slightly more subtle. Hearing his boss at one store gossip about a gay employee at another store stopped him from being open about his own sexuality. This sort of careless gossip can lead many GLBT employees to feel as though their workplace isn't a safe place to work, nor a friendly and secure environment to be themselves.

Sarah, who also worked at a fast-food outlet, experienced more blatant harassment. 'For example, I'd pick up my pay-slip and someone had written "fag" across it. I knew people were talking about me.' Sarah took action by complaining to her store manager, at the same time handing in her resignation. 'I explained what had been happening and that I didn't want to work there as a result. My restaurant manager was quick to ask me not to resign, asking me to give it a couple of weeks until he could sort it out.' When Sarah did return two weeks later, the one person she was definite was involved had been fired. Others whom she'd suspected of being involved had been warned, and the harassment hasn't occurred again.

No matter how difficult a situation at work may become, GLBT young people have to remember that they're not to blame. Discrimination, harassment and abuse in the workplace are illegal. Those who are to blame have to be held accountable. Should this situation arise, both Veronica and Sarah advise young people to take action, be firm and assertive and demand that this treatment cease. There are many avenues of pursuing this action, varying on the degree of severity and circumstances of the harassment. Complaints to the young person's manager or supervisor are usually the first steps to be taken. If the situation isn't taken care of at this level, utilising the services of unions may be the next step.

Although some situations are possibly diffused by the young GLBT person speaking directly to those responsible, many young people fear added confrontation. Young people should never be afraid of telling someone this sort of behaviour is occurring, and should they be afraid for their safety, young people should take care not to place themselves at any added risk. By contacting the police or friends and family who can support them, the young person will send out the signal that this behaviour will not be stood for.

Should the situation be dealt with inappropriately or ineffectively, there are youth-friendly and GLBT-friendly legal representatives and legal organisations that may be able to assist.

Simply ignoring it rarely ever diffuses the situation. Taking assertive action against this behaviour will demonstrate to others that homophobia is unlawful and will not be tolerated, perhaps assisting the prevention of the same perpetrators selecting another target.

Parents challenging homophobia in the workplace

Noel: I work in a heavy industry. There are some homophobic guys around at work. I had one guy come in to my office, look at the photos of my family on my desk, and around my computer, and just say nothing. I tried to talk to him about it but he wasn't willing to. Every time he comes into my office now and sees the photos, he shakes his head and I know he'd like to tell me to get one particular photo off, but he can't. He's sort of hinted it but there's no way I'm going to. My photos of my family are there because I want people to know it's okay to have a gay son.

There's another guy at work whose son's gay and he won't say anything at all, but I have my photos. And every time he comes into the office and sees that I have my photos out, at least he knows someone else is there.

I had another guy who used to come into my office and stir around and say, 'How're you going, poof?' That was his greeting and he thought he was just stirring around, but he was being homophobic. One day he came in and started up about me being a 'poof'. I just turned around and said, 'Well, then, that's why my son is.' He didn't know what to say and of course everybody started laughing and carrying on with him. Later on, he came into the office and actually apologised, 'I'm sorry I called you a poofter.' I knew he was only joking, it was just his terminology. But people think it's okay to do that unless they're taught otherwise. The best part is they start thinking about who else could be gay or have gay kids and hearing this kind of stuff being said.

Karen: There are lots of little things you can do at work. I've got a rainbow mouse pad. I sit in the front office of a school, so that anybody that comes into the school can see this rainbow mouse pad. When we have masses at school I'll wear a rainbow badge. So there's heaps and heaps of little, positive things that you can do to show your support, like not listening to homophobic jokes if you're out at a dinner party or work function – you don't have to identify as having a son or daughter that's GLBT, but you can turn around and say, 'Look, I really object to that. Somebody who's really dear to me is gay, and I don't like that.'

A dad: I work in an office where I put up photos and messages and people happen to read them as they go by. But there was one guy who challenged me and I just said to him, 'John, I need all these family pictures, they're my family.' I found that worked.

Ian: When Jay came out four years ago, I was employed at an electrical contractors' company in the finance department. It was rather a male-dominated company, the father and the sons and the uncles and all that sort of thing, and as Jay was going through a hard time coming out, I guess we were as well. I was trying to come out, wanted to come out, and the way I did it was just before we were going to go to our first Mardi Gras.

It was the Friday night and everyone was going home. As they were going down the steps, I yelled out, 'Watch TV on Sunday night. You might see me.' And that's virtually how I brought it all out in the open. Some of them did see me, and ever since then I've talked about it openly. I used to play cards around the table every lunchtime, and every opportunity I got I'd say something. We'd talk about it, and in the end, it was very open and I felt terrific. There were very, very few who said anything detrimental and I thought it was a positive way of talking to the guys at work. So the more you're out the better for you, and the more you can help other people as well.

A mum: Our daughter has a disability. We had a lot of trouble getting good carers who would be okay with her sexuality. For example, she wanted to go to gay venues and some aides were not prepared to take her to gay events. So we couldn't let them be with her, and that ruled out a couple of agencies. They were not prepared to cater for her sexuality.

Naomi: We had some painters, electricians, plumbers work in our house while we were renovating. If they used homophobic language, we'd request that they not use that language in our home as we found it offensive. In particular, our painter went around calling everything gay when he was grumbling, like, 'That poofter wall's not straight,' and, 'That poofter paint isn't mixing right.' Sure, it might be funny, but it's homophobic. This led to great chats about sexuality, and some coming outs with workers about GLBT members of their own families and friends. We also have rainbow stickers, fridge magnets and Pride posters openly displayed in our home, and this lets anyone who comes in to our home in whatever capacity know how we feel and what we'll expect from them.

Coming out with our kids in rural communities

Margaret Ainsworth

When our daughter Chris came out to us, my husband and I were living in a small country town. We'd shifted up from the suburbs so were newcomers to the area. I was on many committees in the town and I'd always said I was glad people didn't know my children very well as I knew how people talked about other people's children, especially in a small country town. Chris was a very well-known person and I found it very difficult when she came out. I gradually went off committees and kept to myself. I found it very difficult to know who to trust in our small town.

You've got to travel a long distance to meet like-minded people and that was the hardest. I'd heard many times of support groups on many different things so my first thought was to ring the Women's Switchboard and the Gay & Lesbian Counselling Service to find out if there was a support group for parents of gay children, which I found there wasn't. After seven months, through a health centre, I found a counsellor who was a tremendous help to me. I was also trying to get my husband to shift from the rural area. I wanted to move to a place where no-one knew me. I was now having counselling regularly. Even though I came out to some of our family and friends, I still kept to myself.

I joined Women's Health in the local town when Chris was chairperson of the advisory committee. I used to wonder who knew and who didn't know that Chris was a lesbian. I find it much easier now that I can be more out. When I wasn't confident to speak out, I felt so isolated and alone.

When the Adelaide Women's Health Centre decided to start a group for mothers of lesbians, my counsellor ran it for a short time and then I became the coordinator, which was a very interesting and challenging time for me. Chris always took a great interest in what I was doing and her new lesbian friends would come along to the group and tell their stories. The group expanded to provide support to mothers of gay men. After three years, the group expanded again to include fathers.

I don't know if it's my generation but only one of my friends asked me anything about what I was doing or involved in, yet most of them have known Chris all her life. It was a very slow process setting it up, as mothers found it hard to come out and seek help, and it's amazing how someone knows someone else. I wrote an article for the local paper about coming out and 200 copies went out around the rural area, and that's quite a distance, but there wasn't one answer. A lot of cases it's the fear of being outed, of being seen; it stops people getting together.

I really feel for GLBT young people living in the country as I know it's hard to get help where there are no services. I recently experienced a setback. This was after Chris and I appeared in an article in the state's main newspaper. I was reminded that coming out in support of your child who is gay isn't accepted by many. We've got to be courageous. I know I had to do it.

Chris and her mum, Margaret

Parents share their experiences of small town 'outings'

A mum: One of my best girlfriends where I live in a small town – her daughter had been born a man and wanted to be a female. Not only was her daughter ostracised by the churches down there but she eventually attempted suicide. But my friend is now helping a lot of other mothers in the rural area to provide support on suicide.

A mum: My son is gay and HIV positive. I live in a small seaside town and there's no way I can tell many people. I just can't be bothered with the ignorance that surrounds me, especially from, and I hate to say it, churchy people. Now he's got full-blown AIDS, and that's a hell of a journey to go through; you only have so much energy and you don't want to waste it. I'm in constant grief and so much of your time is spent in dealing with this. It's always under the surface and in supporting my son through a journey like AIDS, I cannot be bothered with pettiness.

My son's been incredibly brave and has talked openly to a lot of people who work in mental health and he works with professionals to support others. He's involved in several different organisations. He's made a really positive thing from something quite negative. He's made this a celebration of his life. He's an incredible teacher to me and I can't be bothered with small minds that haven't got a global view. I don't have the energy to stand up in the church with a vicar who has said, 'Well, you all know about AIDS and how that's transmitted.' When I heard that, I just thought, 'Forget it.'

A mum: In small or rural communities, there's a lack of support, support services, openness, people who are accepting. I'm in the Country Women's Association and the choir and there's no way I would come out there. I know that immediately I would be pushed out because I've heard the way they talk. We often support and fund-raise for certain groups and charities and they suggest supporting everything but never HIV/AIDS groups and charities. So, sadly I keep quiet. I'm a bit ashamed of that, but I'm testing the waters. A few friends I have been able to tell.

A mum: When I was at a local community meeting, people were damning homosexuality, so I stood up and spat it out. For a while people looked at me strangely, and now it's not an issue. They know where I stand. But I tried to put information out about meetings people could go to as there are gay people in our community. The local doctor has said to me, 'Can I send someone to speak to you because you're happy to talk about your children's sexuality?' I've put notices on the community noticeboards one day and they'll be gone the next day. Someone will just remove them. So you're up against that sort of thing.

Shirley: I was born and have grown up in a small community and when Shane came out to us, I couldn't wait to tell everybody. I just blabbed to anybody and everybody. Since then, Graham and I have been on television and in the local papers. I've recently had a girlfriend come back home from interstate. We got together for lunch and were catching up on the news and at the end of that she went on to say she's got a gay daughter. We've been friends for years, but now she's back home, she's very selective who she tells because a lot of her friends are very homophobic, and she feels more comfortable talking to me and only very close friends about it. Her daughter's having a baby and she's thrilled to bits about it, but she just can't get out and wave the flag and say, 'My daughter's having a baby,' because there are so many people out there that wouldn't like to know about it. So we're talking about starting our own little group in our local town.

Coming out means coming in to the GLBT community

Like any community, the GLBT community cannot be placed on a pedestal. It's certainly a necessary and fantastic space for GLBT young people to feel great about themselves and enjoy strong cultural, political, social and intimate connections with others. Parents can encourage and support GLBT young people to connect with members of the GLBT community. Drive them to meetings, get-togethers, festivals and other events (and even attend yourself if your young person wants you to!), point out movies and GLBT sections in bookshops. Get them in touch

with GLBT adults who can be great mentors and role models. Introduce them to websites and other online support and social networking, as well as talking to them about Internet safety.

Some parents may feel uncomfortable when their children come out and all they want to do is go to GLBT events, mix only with other GLBT people, and devour GLBT movies, books, magazines, music. Keep in mind that many GLBT young people have had minimal opportunities to learn about GLBT history and cultures, and figure out the place they want to have in their local GLBT community and its culture. Parents who have migrated from another country or moved interstate may recall similar experiences of wanting to find others like yourself, wanting to tap into your own cultural networks and communities, needing to start new friendships with people who may be in similar lines of work or have similar lifestyles. But for a GLBT young person, add the feeling of being ostracised and condemned, and absent from much of mainstream social, political and cultural life, and you'll see why they want to seek out their own safe spaces, places and networks. They want a sense of community and connection they've lacked for too long, and yet is so necessary to the development of mental health and self-esteem.

Connecting with the GLBT community is also necessary to the development of a critical understanding and selective participation in the GLBT community because, unfortunately, like any community, there may be stereotypes, dominant images, expectations and codes a young person will need to negotiate – such as how to dress, how to speak, how much you should weigh, how muscular you should be, how to spend your money, how often to have sex and with whom, how often to engage in drug and alcohol use, which suburb to live in. There is racism, sexism, ableism, classism and internalised homophobia in the gay community. Check out some gay and lesbian community attitudes to bisexual and transgendered people. Some gays and lesbians treat bisexual and transgendered people as if they're beneath them on a ladder of normality – yeah, just like some straights think gays and lesbians are beneath them on a ladder of normality!

Brace yourself to belong

Luke Williams

Meandering
Devastating

My first experience in gay culture.

Trembling

Despite just having my braces removed, my attempt at subscribing to
the gay 'look' fell desperately short of the uniformed ideal. I went to a
nightclub; it was dark, loud, strange. I thought to myself, 'Why stand
around in a stinky, loud pub and listen to music?'

This question seemed to evade my friends who were deeply embed-
ded in atmosphere. I was able to feed a little off their humour, concen-
trating on the contents of their conversation. It was able to sink my
underlying feeling of unease.

But when they left me alone for a desired dance, that I had declined,
my thoughts began to wander, perhaps three times as fast as my eyes.
Boys in dresses, guys who didn't look at all
gay, yuppie types. Could they all be gay?

Fear, anxiety. I think:

'They're looking at me, I bet they think I am really weird, really uncool.'

I felt hot, suffocated, alone, alienated. I asked my friend for the keys to her car, but not before tears had begun to trickle down my cheeks. Falling down my cheeks like the blood from an unconscious cyst bleeding into awareness. It was telling me that these girly boys, leather men and yuppies were a group, I was an outsider.

The Rites of Spring

In the following, Wayne Martino points out that there are, unfortunately, hierarchies of popularity in the GLBT community that replicate the hierarchies in the wider world. His title, 'No fems, fats or Asians', are the kinds of lines found in gay chat rooms on the Internet.

Just when you think you've left a high school where the 'cool' boys and 'cool' girls made your life hell, you might be 'coming in' to a GLBT community where there might be a whole new set of 'cool' boys and 'cool' girls sorting you out in a hierarchy of belonging and not belonging. Sadly, some of those in the gay and lesbian 'cool group' have forgotten what it was like to be classified 'uncool' in the schoolyard. Or maybe this is their way of compensating for it, their own bite of the power pie!

So when coming out, look forward to 'coming in' to the GLBT community, but know that you ultimately have to 'come in' to yourself, your individuality and identity, within that community.

'No fems, fats or Asians' (from a gay chat room!)

Wayne Martino

Often friends and guys I meet tell me they can't stand 'mincy poofs' or 'those queens' who feel they have to go around making a big deal about their sexuality and drawing attention to themselves. 'I want a real man, you know, a guy that acts like a real guy, who's not girlie or queenie.' 'If I wanted a guy who was like a girl I wouldn't be gay then, would I?' Other attitudes are expressed in GLBT forums, such as: 'Straight acting seeks same', 'Stats please'; 'How hung are you?'; and 'Are you a top or a bottom?'

What messages do young guys coming in to the gay community get about what it means to be gay? How does homophobia, sexism and racial discrimination impact on same-sex attracted youth? These are important questions.

What does it actually mean to be gay in the GLBT community? For many it's about sifting through the labels and classifications that drive desire for particular men. 'But that's just the way I am. I just don't like effeminate men,'; 'No fems, no fats, no Asians.' But our desires get caught up in a social system that sorts out and discriminates against certain types of guys. There are those who are defined as desirable and those who are not. This is not somehow 'just natural'.

The assertion of many gay men that they are 'masculine' or 'straight-acting' is often about claiming normalcy or legitimating what it means to be a normal man. Why do so many gay men subscribe to this idea of being 'normal'? Maybe it's got to do with power and how male power gets eroticised. Just a thought! The idea that being gay is somehow linked to deviancy, to being more like a woman than a real man, is still quite a powerful notion in our culture. The links between effeminacy and failed masculinity are still alive and well.

Coming into the gay community for many men is to hold on to a valued straight-acting masculinity. This may be to compensate on a deep or unconscious level for feeling inferior in the wider world on the basis of identifying as gay: 'I might be gay but I'm still a real man!' To be effeminate or to be associated with the feminine in any way is degrading. As Madonna tells us in her song, 'What It Feels Like For a Girl', girls can wear traditional male clothing and cut their hair short because being a boy is okay. But for a boy to wear traditional women's clothing and make-up is not okay because to be a girl is 'degrading'. All of this is often about hierarchies among men, with 'straight acting', 'gym-toned' or 'real men' at the top of the social ladder and those 'mincy poofs' or 'fem' guys at the bottom.

Maybe we can start asking questions from the inside of the community: 'What does it mean to be gay? What does it mean to be a man? Who decides what is normal? How can we learn to embrace diverse ways of being male, of being gay, outside of a social system that sorts guys into hierarchical positions on a social ladder? Aren't we just emulating or imitating what straight men do when we behave like this?'

I believe we can still address the homophobia that exists on the outside, while at the same time looking at how we learn to relate to and treat other men on the inside.

Coming out and being disabled: risky business
Tony

Having a physical disability and being GLBT is more common than most people imagine. Indeed, people with disabilities are considered, by the wider community, to be far less sexual than we really are. Of course, people with disabilities are just as likely as anyone else to have sexual feelings for a person of the same sex.

Having a disability can make coming out even harder for a young person, especially when there is a dependence on caregivers who may hold negative attitudes towards GLBT sexualities. Consider, for example, a young gay man with cerebral palsy who lives with his parents. He depends on them for his primary care and has heard them make negative references to gays and lesbians his whole life. At one time he heard his father say, 'I think all gays should be put on an island and shot!' How does this young man tell his parents that he is gay? While he will feel similar fears of rejection and abandonment to those experienced by non-disabled GLBT youth, he will also fear losing his primary care and being institutionalised.

A dependence on others for care also makes the exploration of a person's sexuality and the gay and lesbian community more difficult. This early exploration is usually achieved privately and independently, at a time when the person feels a sense of apprehension and cautiousness. The non-disabled person can do this with minimal risk and with little fear of their family and friends knowing. However, a person with a disability may need support to attend a gay venue, such as support with transport, communication or personal care. This often requires negotiation and disclosure and the need to come out at a time when the person may not feel prepared or confident. Furthermore, physical access to the venue also needs to be considered.

For a person with a disability, coming out requires a great deal of courage and risk taking. I remember finding the process overwhelming. The only way I could manage this was to break it down into tasks that seemed achievable. My initial step involved calling a city GLBT community centre, after hearing about their service on a talkback radio program. It took many attempts before I could keep my anxiety at bay for long enough to dial the full number. I spoke to the coordinator, who suggested I attend a young men's group that met in the inner city.

I found the idea of attending this group terrifying. Again, I broke the task down. I looked for how to get there, undertook a practice run and then on a fine April day, I entered the centre and said, 'Hi, is this the young men's group?' I was overwhelmed by anxiety and fear. I was so conscious of my disability. No-one else in the room had a visible impairment. I thought I would be shunned and rejected because of my physical disability. I did not feel as 'sexy' as the others. Some in the group treated me poorly at times but others were very welcoming and I enjoyed the sharing, the joking and the novelty of the experience. It was great to be in a space where it was okay to be gay. I made some wonderful friends and had some great experiences including some party nights on the gay scene. Within two years I became convener of the group and I continued in this role for several more years.

As people with disabilities, we are constantly faced with barriers and discrimination in almost all facets of life. Some people will wish that our sexuality did not exist or that we would keep quiet about it. Speaking out and coming out involves a high degree of risk when you rely on others for your survival. Sometimes we take risks and survive. Sometimes we're glad we took the chance. Other times we wish we had kept quiet. Either way, we want to be loved for who we are – disabled, queer, whatever!

Being GLBT and 'ethnic'

Many GLBT young people from diverse cultural backgrounds experience feelings of inhabiting 'cultural borderlands'. They're on the borders of, and want to belong to, several communities:

▶▶ their ethnic communities within which they may experience homophobia

▶▶ their predominantly Anglo GLBT community within which they may experience racism

▶▶ the predominantly Anglocentric heteronormative society within which they may experience both racism and homophobia.

In this section, let's hear how GLBT young people negotiate these borders and what can be done so that they can rightfully belong to all their communities.

'I was really scared jumping into the queer scene': Yellowkitties talk racism in the GLBT community

T: I was really scared to just jump into the queer scene. I thought everyone would eat me. You just need courage to tell people. To go to the scene and just check things out. See similar kinds of people and feel comfortable.

Charmaine: I would probably be more inclined to put my ethnic community at the forefront, regardless of the fact I'm a lesbian. I feel like it's quite exclusive in the lesbian scene, in terms of the white women. I bring a lot of my loyalties to my ethnic community.

Lian: I've been in situations where I've been very conscious about being the only Asian woman in the room. Having a group like Yellowkitties – which is an Asian lesbian social support group – helps in a way.

T: That's a good way to empower lots of us.

Lian: Yeah, like doing social things or going out to venues together. It's a group of us, and it's fun. It's supportive. It's this unspoken understanding about all of who we are.

T: Because there's subtle racism everywhere. Like you get asked constantly, 'Where are you from?'

Charmaine: I get asked that all the time.

T: Or they say, 'Your English is really good.' Because I'm a foreigner I can take those questions. But if you're a second-generation Asian woman born in this country, who's never been overseas even, how would you feel?

Charmaine: It's that exclusiveness in the gay and lesbian community. I find that here even with my own friends. Pretty much most of them are white. I've got one friend that's part-Singaporean. She's probably the only other woman of colour. She's lighter than me. I find that whenever I go out, you're really tokenised because of your culture. Within even the lesbian community, I have people come up to me and say, 'Can you speak Indian?' There's no such thing as Indian anyway. Really stupid stuff. That's probably the less insulting part of it. I get asked all the time, 'Do you know the *Karma Sutra*?'

T: Well, I get questions about *Memoirs of a Geisha* all the time.

Charmaine: Yeah, it's sexualising and exoticising us because we happen to be from that culture. The *Karma Sutra* is a book on the art of love, of making love. It was written in Hindi a long time ago. So you sort of turn around and say, 'I wrote the book!' Because if you take it to heart, you just get so disillusioned, so angry. And these people are just ignorant. It probably wasn't meant to offend you. But it does.

Lian: People don't understand where our anger is coming from.

Charmaine: I go out places where white women are wearing saris and I can't get over that. Or have the 'tika-tika'. That's really fashionable. It's like, 'Wow, it's so hippy and cool.' Total appropriation of culture. That doesn't sit well with me because I just find it's not their place. To me it's almost like making fun of it. And also it's very righteous. Like they have a right to do it. I find it's a bit presumptuous.

Lian: I think that there's a difference when there's a respect there, and trying to find out the whole history, specifically where it's come from, rather than wear something because it's part of a popular thing to do and be totally disrespectful.

Expressing my gayness with an Italian flavour
Vittorio Perri

In my teenage years it was becoming increasingly difficult to be constantly reminded by my family that I was Italian while at the same time I was trying to fit in with an Anglo-dominated environment. I was torn between two worlds. I began to resent this situation. I felt like the Italian thing was constantly shoved down my throat by my very proud nationalistic dad. Every time we had an argument I dealt with it by disowning my Italian heritage.

This unworkable paradigm became even more problematic when I began to have 'those' feelings. Those feelings of knowing that I wasn't quite what my parents wanted of me. The standard mantra, 'Of course you'll get married and have kids!', began to grind at me. I had these feelings that I knew deep down were not compatible with the future my father had expected for me. What a huge secret and burden I had.

As I approached nineteen I began to think I just couldn't be the only one in this whole world that felt the way I did. I discovered a newsagent in the city that had gay magazines and newspapers. I flicked through the newspapers and found a couple of advertisements for gay venues. A whole range of mixed feelings would overwhelm me just looking at the ads. I felt excited that there could be places where I could meet other guys just like myself and I felt nervous and anxious about what these places would be like, and of walking alone into a pub or bar full of strangers, having all these eyes stare at me.

I was extremely anxious the first time I approached a gay club. I walked in and was just amazed at what I saw. I'd never seen so many men like me together in one gathering. Naturally many eyes were on me since I was a new face. This started to make me feel uncomfortable and I started to panic. I thought, 'Who knows, they could all gang up on me and rape me or something.' I just couldn't handle it so I left after only ten minutes. I did that twice before feeling comfortable enough to stick it out.

However nervous I was, that first experience was a godsend. I no longer felt I was the only guy who felt this way. I found a space with other gay men where I could express myself more freely. I had my family, even though they still didn't know, but I also had an outlet that involved other people where I could express my sexuality.

But something wasn't quite right. And I didn't even know what the issue was till I found the solution. While I felt this new freedom in this gay environment and began new gay friendships, I began to realise I was still incomplete as a person. I still could not express myself totally even with my new friends. While the first problem I had was that I couldn't tell my family about my sexuality, now I couldn't comfortably express my cultural background with my new gay friends. Sure I'd always get the obvious stuff like 'Italian Stallion'. The reputation that Italians are supposed to be hot in bed certainly becomes an advantage if one is into casual sex. However, when trying to have some serious conversation with my Anglo friends about some of the issues I had to deal with at home, they'd laugh. It would usually be a disinterested 'big deal'. 'Yeah, yeah we all have it hard at home.' Yes it can be hard regardless of background but I had extra issues that I had to deal with coming from an ethnic background. I felt I was getting from my friends a more subtle form of racism.

I remember going out one night to a gay bar and I ran into a friend from the same background. An Italian background. He was there with a couple of other guys who also happened to be from an Italian background. Then one of them spotted another friend in the crowd who was also from the same background. My friend spotted someone else. There were even more in the crowd and before we knew it there we were about a dozen of us all drinking together in a group. We were all gay men with the same cultural background. It was an amazing experience. I'd never felt like that before. Not in a gay environment and definitely not at home. It seemed a subconscious thing as well that as we spoke English for the general conversation we would then break into Italian when we wanted to be humorous, particularly swear words or the phrases that your parents used when they told you off. Every time someone would say one we laughed. It felt strange talking Italian like this in a gay club, but it also felt good.

All I could think about for days was that night. I'd never felt so truly open about my feelings before. I was able to express my gayness with an Italian flavour and have total empathy from a group around me. At home I couldn't be gay. On the scene I couldn't be too ethnic. But that night I was with these guys being both. It was an experience that was probably not going to happen often enough. So a bunch of us got together and thought, 'Why not start up some sort of support/social group?'

The Southern European and Latin Gay Men's Group was born. We first met at a friend's place for dinner, a private and safe environment. Without the distractions of a dance club and being in a gay environment where admittedly one would feel more self-conscious, we were really able to seriously discuss the issues that we had with our families.

The group continued for a few years with regular meetings. The direct value of the group for ourselves in terms of peer support was there but there was an indirect benefit as well. We realised that as a group we could potentially change racist attitudes in the wider GLBT community. We'd participate in major community events, particularly festivals, where we'd have a stall with information about our group.

We also organised some events of the likes that the GLBT community had never seen before. One of the events we organised were pasta busts at a gay bar. While the traditional beer busts allowed you to pay a certain amount and then have all the beer and wine you wanted to drink and a hot dog, our twist was that we provided all the beer and wine for you to drink plus a bowl of spaghetti bolognese. And we'd even make it fresh on the spot. Needless to say, we were a hit! We also organised tram parties with Italian folk songs blaring out of the speakers, and weekends away.

A few years later the AIDS Council/Gay Men's Health Centre started to support gay men's groups that came from culturally and linguistically diverse backgrounds such as the Italian & Gay Network, the Greek & Gay Network, the Arab & Gay group, the South Asian & Gay group. It's great that these groups exist.

Some of my family are Italian, and the other side is English. My son sat down one day at a Christmas table, about twenty of us, and he just said, 'I'm gay, and proud of it,' and showed everyone this great T-shirt with a rainbow on it. They all accepted it really nicely, my Italian mother being the best, and she's 85. **A mum**

Will you choose your children or your community?

Karla Mokros

I come from Czechoslovakia. We've got two children, a boy and a girl. Jindrich is 24. He was five and Wendy was three when we came to Australia. Jindrich was twenty when he came out.

We've got no friends anymore in our Czech community because they honestly think we are bad parents. They think we should stop our son from being gay. The gossip spread among Czech people because my husband sometimes goes with Jindrich to a gay bar for a drink, and they told him that they'd seen him at a gay place. Certainly somebody from our community has been there as well otherwise people wouldn't know he's there! So gossip and rejection keep us from being involved in the Czech community. Our closest friends now try to avoid us. It's supposed to be our community but it's not, and we've got a few friends from different nationalities.

I think the Czech people here come from a very suppressed community, where people either think homosexuality doesn't exist or believe gay people are to be laughed at, and that they are really not acceptable. Today, Prague has actually opened the door and is catering to gay tourists. They've got so many restaurants and cafes. They're tolerant to the tourists who actually come with the dollars. But what happens to gay Czech people, when others are still being very offensive toward them, saying they deserve to be in gaol? I remember we had two female teachers who never married. They lived together and we called them 'old maids', but it didn't enter anyone's head that they could be two lesbians. I had a girlfriend who actually lived with her mum and 'aunty'. And because it was mum and aunty, everybody was really so kind to them but it would be different if they'd actually come out about who they really were.

We wonder if our relatives in Czechoslovakia know about Jindrich.

A friend of my son was in Czechoslovakia and was introduced to a girl who came to Australia and lived with us for six months, thinking she would marry Jindrich. He took her to gay pubs but she thought, 'No, he can't be gay, he just knows so many nice boys.' When they actually told her that she couldn't marry him, she was very, very upset and very angry. It would be interesting to know what she actually came up with back in Czechoslovakia. We never hear from anyone, but certainly when she got home, she would've said, 'Oh, he's a fag.' Jindrich should go for a holiday to Prague because it's so cheap and beautiful. He says he'd like to go over and discuss these things with relatives there, to come out, to say, 'I'm gay and that's it.' It would be interesting what my parents and relatives would say.

Many migrants never actually master English so they never read any books in English. They still live in a small ethnic community, reading ethnic papers, and these don't tell them much about homosexuality. Maybe if my son hadn't been gay, I might've been one of them, judging my friend's children and wondering how they can accept homosexuality. So it's given me an enormous chance to be tolerant and look at people in a different way. Even my work in the social work department of a hospital has benefited. I come across so many different people who you have to accept. I'm able to accept so many people, even religious fundamentalists! I'm so open to people's family issues and problems.

There should be more education for ethnic communities, but nobody who is actually involved in the Czech community will come out. I know about one family that has a gay daughter, and they actually told us she's getting married. I feel so sorry for them but they are Christian fundamentalists, and homosexuality is not permitted. I also used to counsel an ethnic woman who had breast cancer. She actually said to me her son was homosexual and her specific ethnic community would never accept it. I told her about my situation, but she suicided before I could continue talking to her. I'd given her my telephone number and then I heard she took her life. I don't know if it was her illness or her son's homosexuality or both combined.

Judging by the statistics, there must be an enormous number of migrant people who are having the same experiences. I did a little bit of research into Czech literature and resources for migrants and found nothing on homosexuality. So I want to tell my story to my ethnic community. I'm not ashamed to actually let people know that these things are not some science fiction. I just think many people don't know what to do and they suffer alone. Many kids can't get out. I know a few of my son's friends whose parents have got no idea what's going on and I just think it's a real shame. People are forced to live a lie. In my country, people must marry and then they meet each other somewhere secretly, and this must be really, really difficult. So I admire my son for coming out.

I don't feel ashamed in front of anybody from our community, not at all. We had a few phone calls in Czech language. One phone call was from a young man about my son being part of a gay and lesbian festival. This was published in a gay glossy magazine, which I'd never seen before. This young man said very, very nasty things like: 'Your poofter son, he's in this gay magazine.' I was really worried about what kind of magazine it was and I asked my son to bring it home. I was thinking it was some really pornographic magazine, but it was a photo of his face and a description of the music and songs which they were singing. I was more than angry with that young man. I feel sorry for people like him who make those phone calls. And I can believe somebody who has a problem coming out using this way to attack others. I actually said, 'If you want, we can meet.' And he just said, 'No.' Another incident was when our son was part of a bridal party and when they found out he was gay they cut him off.

We have a great relationship with Jindrich. He could move away and never come home and we'd never know where he was. This is what happens to many parents of gay kids if they don't love their children. To other ethnic parents going through this, I ask you to just think about the courage your child has to come out to you. They risk so much, and it shows an enormous trust they have in their parents if they do it. They must trust it will end well and they deserve to be treated well. And it doesn't matter how bad it is for parents, it actually will work out. You never know how unconditional love can be until you are there. You can be very accepting but I don't think anybody has looked into the pram and said, 'Well, I can't wait until my son grows up into a really nice, beautiful gay man.' Society doesn't prepare you for that or even lead you to think about it.

So we are no longer part of our ethnic community, but we have actually become part of another community, the gay community.

Karla with son Jindrich and
her husband

Working with GLBT young people and their ethnic communities

Mic Emslie

Community projects for GLBT young people need to consider and work with differing cultural meanings and aspects of sexuality. As community workers, we need to:

1. increase our own understandings of the ways in which diverse cultural backgrounds shape GLBT young people's experience of their sexuality

2. explore ways to make our projects accessible, relevant and responsive to young people from diverse ethnic and racial communities

3. promote our projects within ethnic organisations, religious and cultural groups, in ethnic media, and among people who work with young people from culturally diverse communities.

Here are some ideas that help meet these aims:

Access to culturally appropriate information

▶▶ GLBT young people lack access to culturally sensitive information and support. Find out about their familial and cultural values and understandings of sexuality and then develop responses that are sensitive to these beliefs and ideas.

▶▶ Not all people share Western ideas regarding sexuality. In particular, everyone does not define sexual behaviour in the framework of heterosexuality, homosexuality and bisexuality. In some cultures there are actually no meanings or words for same-sex relations and emotions. Therefore, the concepts 'gay', 'lesbian', 'bisexual' and 'transgender' can be very alien to some people, particularly those who are newly arrived in the country or part of emerging migrant populations.

▸▸ Provide information to young people from ethnic communities about the ways GLBT identities are formed and lived in their familial country of origin. Information can be obtained from:

  ▸▸ the Internet
  ▸▸ international and national organisations and services
  ▸▸ libraries.

▸▸ Assumptions based on race or ethnicity should not be made about who someone is, what someone is, or what their experience is. Some families and communities are very accepting and supportive.

Coming out and staying in

Two issues for some GLBT young people from culturally diverse communities are:

1. How can I live the life I want (e.g. as an open GLBT person in a same-sex relationship) and still fit in with my family and community?

2. What happens to me if I'm disconnected from my family due to my sexuality?

Coming out is constructed as a big landmark for the GLBT community in Western countries, but isn't necessarily so for all people from ethnic communities. In family and other gatherings involving people from their families' country of origin, a GLBT identity may remain unspoken. But it isn't necessarily unrecognised – for example, people may be invited to bring their same-sex partner to a family function, but being lesbian or gay will not be spoken about. It shouldn't be expected or assumed that young people from ethnic communities will want to come out as GLBT to their families or people from their familial country of origin.

The development of responses to support GLBT young people from diverse communities should take into account the ways in which coming out may impact on their families (e.g. it may bring shame to the family), and how people from different cultures may understand someone in their family coming out (e.g. it may represent bad karma for the family).

Barriers to accessing the mainstream GLBT community

The disadvantaged socio-economic position of many young people from ethnic communities often means that they lack the disposable income generally required to access the mainstream GLBT community.

Lack of fluency in English can be a barrier to young people from ethnic communities accessing groups for GLBT young people.

Newly arrived migrant and refugee young people often come with a history of traumatic experiences. This can limit the significance of sexuality issues in their lives.

Responding to homophobia among young people from culturally and linguistically diverse communities

1. There are differences within cultural and religious groups concerning sexuality and gender, ranging from anti-homophobic to extremely homophobic. We must avoid stereotyping all ethnic youth as homophobic, as well as understand how homophobic behaviour may be an attempt by young ethnic men to gain some measure of power and superiority.

2. There are cultural differences in the way young people learn about sexual diversity. For example, some young people may be more receptive to educational approaches, while others may only come to understand that homophobia is not acceptable through religious values of love, compassion, acceptance and respect for individuals.

3. The ways in which ethnic communities and their leaders may respond to anti-homophobic programs should be considered, and their support gained if possible.

Networking with ethnic communities

There are key organisations that work with ethnic groups and ethnic young people which can provide information and resources. These include peak non-government and government health and welfare services, as well as regional and local organisations, which can also provide support and information. For example:

- migrant resource centres

- centres for ethnicity and health

- English language schools

- immigrant women's services

- Foundation for the Survivors of Torture and Trauma

- AIDS Council/Gay Men's Health Service.

The appropriate contact person may be the youth worker, student welfare coordinator or settlement worker. Some organisations also have people who work with people from specific ethnic communities.

Coming out in religious communities

I'm driving around in my old brown car. I pull up at a traffic light, and the guy in the car next to me winds down his window and yells out, 'Faggot lover! You've got the devil in the car with you!'

I have rainbow stickers – 'PFLAG: Keeping Families Together' and 'Unity in Diversity' – on my rear windscreen

He roars off as the lights change. He has 'Jesus Lives' and the Peace Dove on his rear windscreen.

I receive a letter from a mother. She bought my books for her adolescent children only to find that I am 'promoting sin' and 'Satanism' by 'encouraging young people to be sexual perverts'. As a 'good Christian mother' she burnt them before her children could get to them.

I feel an incredible pain on behalf of the beautiful young people in those books. It's like she's burned them. In another time in history, she might've been able to.

I write back to her, expressing my hope that as 'a good Christian mother', should her own children ever come out as gay, or experience the devastation so many of the GLBT young people I work with experience, that she'll love and affirm them … not burn them.

You're not God's mistake

A dad: No homosexual person deserves an ill-informed priest with flames coming out of his nostrils.

A mum: You just need to take one person and they will go to another person and then you have two. If you educate two people, they will go and educate five people and then you have seven. You can keep educating individual people like this in your local parishes. The most important thing is information and education.

A gay son: Many gay kids don't keep their religion because they can't connect their sexuality to religious homophobia. I still go. I mean, I'm the church organist, and I don't have any problems. I've been going to Acceptance for GLBT Catholics for a number of years and I'm very, very actively involved. If anyone hassles me, I say, 'Look, God didn't make mistakes. End of story. Any other idea is all just man made. God didn't make mistakes.'

Isabella: I've got a friend who's a Pentecostal pastor. She was the first person who I actually told about my son. She said to me, 'I will pray for him to change.' I said to her, 'I really don't want that. It would be a disaster. I don't think anybody can ever change you. If you'd like to pray for him, just pray for him to be accepted and to be happy.' She tried hard. She even invited us for Christmas dinner, even my son with his partner, and I so wanted my son to come. But they never accepted what he is and it's sad because they've got a congregation with very young families, lots of children, and I ask her, 'How will you deal with it when people come out and say, our children are gay? How will your church actually deal with that?' She said to me, 'Well, Isabella, I love the person, but hate the sins.' I can't understand how you can divide a person like this. I don't think it's possible.

A mum: When my daughter came out to her church after being very involved, we had people who rang up to say if they'd known she was going to be gay, she wouldn't have been allowed to do what she was involved in. Definitely not a Christian attitude. And so we don't go to church.

Bernadette: I've actually challenged my parish priest about this. To start off with, I got angry. I was watching all of these beautiful communicants, eight and nine-year-olds; there must've been sixty of them, all standing on the altar, and I got to thinking, 'There's got to be some of them that are gay.' I had to walk out of my mass service and wait until the end of it, because I was really angry. And so, when the priest came outside, I told him I was really angry with him. 'Some of these children you're going to push away and say they're horrible, they're bad and all this sort of stuff.' I was ready for a fight on my hands. He said, 'What's your problem? Everybody's welcome at my table. We don't all believe in what the hierarchy of the Catholic Church think.' And then he got books for me. I've had people in my parish come and talk to me, 'I've got gay children too.' And so by being open and not being ashamed of who your child is, I've opened doors in my religious community.

Hayden: Being Anglican and being a server, and being really involved with the church, it was really hard for me to come out to the whole parish. Most of them were old people who knew me from when I was young, and therefore there were expectations about me they wanted to believe in. It felt a little bit easier when we had a change of priest because the person who's now our priest was very helpful. He was very encouraging and easy to talk to, and I was able to come out in front of him, and also to the rest of my friends when I was up serving. Everyone was more supportive at the younger age. I just couldn't believe how many people in my church community understand.

Jean: I had an occasion where a young heterosexual male at a Christian meeting said he felt really threatened and worried at uni because some of the guys there were homosexual. Suddenly there were eyes popping all around the room when me, this very reserved old lady, stood up and said to this young man, 'You mean if you met a good looking girl and she wasn't interested in you, that you'd rape her? Is that what you mean? Is that what you're insinuating, that homosexual people go around raping other people when they like them?'

Pam: I can be myself at church, often attending with my partner and having people recognise our relationship as they do the many heterosexual couples in the church. I've had the opportunity to write for our church newsletter, challenging and encouraging people to think about who they are and how they respond to others, particularly those who appear 'different'. Much of this has been very scary but I have been, and continue to be, privileged to see the head and heart of Christ leading.

Jo: I grew up in a Chinese Christian community, the mischievous daughter of an inscrutable pastor. I was beginning to think that Christianity had nothing to offer me as a young, dare I say 'hip', lesbian of mixed cultural influences. Fortunately I discovered a whole bunch of people who were serious about their faith and yet interested in things like social justice and cultural diversity.

Nan: We were very, very involved in our parish. There wasn't a parish group that didn't have a McGregor in it. So when Kieran came out, I turned to our church for support and received none. I said to a friend, somebody with whom I'd served on a parish committee, that Kieran was gay. She looked at me with very big eyes and said, 'Oh, you poor unfortunate. What a terrible cross to have to bear in life.' And I thought, 'Oh, dear, are we on the same wavelength?' Then we found that we were slowly being ostracised within the parish because as a family we'd been pretty outspoken. We'd done a few interviews in the papers and on TV and nobody would sit in the same church row as us. It was terribly painful, so we got a bit defiant. We didn't have rainbow sashes in those days, but we had red AIDS memorial ribbons, and the whole lot of us used to sit up in mass with our red AIDS ribbons on.

There were two women who went to church at that particular time who were also getting the cold treatment. Kieran said to me, 'They're lesbian nuns, you know.' And I said, 'They're not lesbian nuns, Kieran.'

'Oh yes, they are.'

'How do you know?'

'I just know.'

Well, it turned out they were not lesbian nuns, but they were in fact lesbians, and I got to know them. They were two beautiful women, and they said that we were the only ones who ever spoke to them in all of their time of going to that church.

Just before this Easter I met this friend of mine who had been a very homophobic churchgoer when Kieran came out. I was doing my grocery shopping, and one and a half hours later we're still talking, and the subject of Kieran came up. She said, 'He's so happy, isn't he?'

'Yes, he is. He's really very, very happy.'

'Oh, I saw the photograph of him and his partner in the paper.' And she looked at me, and her eyes were all swimming with tears. 'How can you ever forgive me?'

So, that was a really lovely thing to happen at Easter time, and yeah, we had a big hug.

Laurene: I was at a Rainbow Sash march and our parish priest saw me on television and said, 'Laurene, I saw you on TV on Sunday night. Good on you.'

God loves the gay me

Johnathan Jones

When I was thirteen years old I became a Bible-bashing, filled with the
Spirit, Pentecostal Christian. I loved the church. I needed the church.
It was my home, the one place where I belonged. It was, and still is,
my greatest love. I knew that I would live my life serving the church.

In my church you married young, you married as a virgin. So, I married at eighteen. On the third day of our honeymoon, I realised I was gay.

We were in an old country town pub. I noticed the waiter and
couldn't stop looking at him. I was attracted to him, captivated by
him. My mind froze, I couldn't think. It was too much.

I had as much sex as I possibly could with my new wife. Whenever
we had a chance, we did it. I was determined, adamant, stubborn.
No, *I am not gay*! I decided I was going to fight my 'homosexual ten-
dencies'.

We joined an ex-gay ministry. Designed to cure you of your sin. I was
going to be set free from the bondage and demons of homosexuality.
I always knew that homosexuality was sinful. More than that, it was
evil. As a Pentecostal, I believed that I was probably possessed by a
devil. I needed God to deliver me. There was a weekend retreat, a
gathering of ex-gays, where we were to encourage one another, help
each other, heal each other. However, it was at this place where I found
I was still very attracted to men.

Three months later I left my wife. I was giving up. I couldn't be
straight, God wouldn't heal me, God had abandoned me. He was a
bastard, I hurt, I cried, I was alone … where was the God who loved
everyone? Why didn't God love me enough to heal me?

I walked along the beach. It was night. I could hear the roar of the
waves, taste the salt in the air, I saw the stars and thought, 'God is so
good to have created all these beautiful things,' and then I realised. It
was as clear as day. God had created me. God had created black-hair
Johnathan, big-smile Johnathan, *gay Johnathan*. God had created me,
and he definitely didn't need to heal me.

It may sound unbelievable, but then I heard the very voice of God:
'Not only did I create you gay, but I love you gay, I want you to be gay,
I want you to be the best gay guy that you can. And I want you to

help others like yourself … let them know that I love them.'

I now work with the Metropolitan Community Church (MCC). We are a denomination that openly supports, affirms and ordains GLBT people. We believe that Jesus loves all people, unconditionally. He never said one has to be straight to trust in him; we just need to believe.

I am the youth pastor at MCC. I tell young people that it is great to be GLBT, that God loves them, and that we, as a church, are here to support them. I encourage them to explore their sexuality and their spirituality. I show them a God of love, rather than hate, a God who wants them and loves them as they are.

We hold special youth worship services, coordinate art and literary exhibitions to encourage young GLBT expression, run camps and retreats, and we offer counselling services for coming out. We give love and friendship to those who often don't receive it. We provide a home.

I love being gay; I don't want to be any other way. I also love God, and I know that God loves me back. God loves me for all of me, the silly me, the happy me, the cranky me, the dreaming me, and most of all God loves … the gay me.

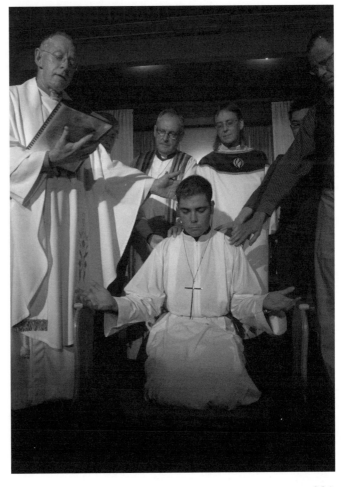

Johnathan being ordained (Photo courtesy of Jamie Dunbar)

Epilogue

Our kids trailblazing ahead

Little Apple

Lauren

They say the apple doesn't fall far from the tree
just rolls downhill and into the stream
carried by the current into the sea
washing up on some distant beach.
The trail I blaze must be my own
even if it means that I walk alone
staring into the vast unknown
crying my tears until I've grown.
I know it's hard to let it end
but for me this is where it begins
watching the trail go around the bend
wondering if it'll come around again.
So as I leave don't cry for me
the little apple floating in the sea
taking pains just to be free
doing what I know is right for me.

You've been on such a journey in this book. One message that's been there throughout, weaving in and out, has been the importance of coming in to yourself, your truths and realities, your beauty and strength, your agency and potential: as a young GLBT person, as a parent or other family member, as a teacher, youth worker, community leader, religious leader.

When all else fails, take care of the self
Agnes Lichtor

The self – a young person's thoughts, feelings, beliefs, views and values – are each as unique as a fingerprint. This individuality makes each and every young person beautiful in their own way, each with a valuable contribution to make to society. Teachers, parents, religious leaders and extended family often reinforce this when the young person is a child, promising them that the world is their oyster.

Then something happens.

The child slowly realises that they are 'different' from other children. From then on, a wonderful and at times frightening period begins, a period of self-examination, self-awareness and the exploration of that new concept: sexuality.

'There were times I became my own counsellor.' (Richard)

Educate yourself even if the world won't educate you.

By educating themselves, GLBT young people have the ammunition against ignorance when confronted by negative and inappropriate reactions. Education about religion, history and culture can help a GLBT young person realise for themselves that there's nothing wrong with being same-sex attracted, or attracted to both sexes, or experiencing personality and emotions likened to both sexes.

'At times, I was my own best friend. From the time I was little, I was always watching, observing people. I became my own ally. When asked if I'm gay, I would say I'm not a gay man, I am a man who is gay and other things like El Salvadorean. I think education is one of the most powerful tools we have. Even when I was little, I would always read, and think. I would just sit there and think for hours. I still do.' (Dave)

A strong spiritual belief structure assists many young GLBT people questioning the validity of their emotions.

'Ever since I could remember, I knew I liked both men and women. I would get funny tingles and ripples down my spine when a nice girl or guy would talk to me. And I was always okay. I am a very spiritual person, I love meditation, contemplation and quiet prayer.' (Jaimie)

Knowing the self and affirming the self are the first key steps in a lifelong journey. The phrase 'before you expect others to love you, you must love yourself' takes on a special meaning here.

Feel positive about yourself
YGLAM Youth Group

– I think as long as you're positive about yourself and start giving out positive vibes you'll deal with any homophobia because unfortunately there'll always be some and it's a product of misjudgement and ignorance and can affect you personally. So take care to feel positive about yourself.

– I suppose the great thing about going through those issues, even if they're traumatic, is that you'll ultimately be a better person. Once you can get through them and just decide to be yourself, and there's people that can't do that even if they're heterosexual, then it's pretty much a big change in your life.

Two Continuous Journeys

Jess Heerde

I've wandered a continuous journey
A journey I've endlessly floated along.
It was someone else's journey,
Someone else's path of wants and expectations.
A continuous journey now ended.

For the first time I feel like me,
No more is the journey unknown
I know who I am and where I want to be,
There is a new journey mapped, however not by other's boundaries
But by personal goals and wants.

A new person,
A fresh start.
The future is still uncertain however
But a new life has begun.
A life without domination of the past.

I start a new journey,
No more continuous wandering.
No more continuous floating.
This is my journey – my wants
    and expectations,
A new continuous journey begun.

Photos courtesy of
Dianne Jeffrey

Author's notes

Page 37: The Coming Out checklist is based on the *Intergalactic Guide to Relationships*, Central Coast Health, NSW.

Page 63: For children raised in anti-homophobic families, see Jennings, Kevin with Shapiro, Pat (2003), *Always My Child: A Parent's Guide to Understanding Your Gay, Lesbian, Bisexual, Transgendered or Questioning Son or Daughter*. New York: Fireside Books.

Page 63: For 'anticipatory socialisation', see Robert K. Merton (1976) *Sociological Ambivalence and Other Essays*. New York: Free Press.

Page 75: The poem by 'Aunty Lois' was published in Parents Supporting Parents FLAG (SA) resource materials for parents.

Page 84: Abe Whyte's 'If I Were A Teacher' is edited and reprinted with kind permission of Dr Lori Beckett and Abe's mum, Rose. The original text is in Lori's 1998 book, *Everyone is Special! A Handbook For Teachers on Sexuality Education*, Brisbane: Association of Women Educators.

Page 101: PFLAG – Parents, Families and Friends of Lesbians and Gays, Inc. – is a support, education and advocacy organisation. See 'PFLAG Contacts'.

Page 165 : Jen Blyth's article was first published in *Purple Bus*, a magazine for same-sex attracted young people by same-sex attracted young people. For more information, contact purplebuszine@hotmail.com.

Page 218: Jo and Pam's pieces excerpted from *Coming Out Alive*, edited by Rev. Rod Pattenden, with kind permission of Rod Pattenden.

Page 219: The Rainbow Sash Movement is an organisation of Gay and Lesbian Catholics, with their families and friends, who are calling for a conversion of heart in the Church around its treatment of gay people. For more information on the Rainbow Sash Movement, see www.rainbowsash.com.

PFLAG Contacts

PFLAG (Parents, Families and Friends of Lesbians and Gays, Inc.) is a support, education and advocacy organisation. Founded in 1981 by 25 parents in the United States, PFLAG now represents more than 60,000 households and speaks for thousands of others. If you'd like to know more about PFLAG, go to www.pflag.org,
http://www.nd.edu/~scglsn/pflag.html
and to
http://www.rainbowquery.com/cgi/rq.exe?ep=cl&cn=358&sp=&lc=0
for listings of many US groups.
All PFLAG websites are listed at http://www.critpath.org/pflag-talk/chaptweb.htm

An example of a New Zealand group is at
http://au.geocities.com/pflagsouth/

For Canadian sites, go to http://www.pflag.ca/chapters.html

Lists of international PFLAGs – e.g. France, UK, Canada, Israel, South Africa – can be found at
http://www.critpath.org/pflag-talk/chapext.htm
and at http://www.critpath.org/pflag-talk/chapintl.htm

Australia

PFLAG Sydney Northside
Phone 02 9949 2743 (Jill) or 02 9939 7706 (Maree)

PFLAG Penrith (Sydney far west and Blue Mountains)
Phone 02 4730 4660 (Vicki) or 02 4735 4680 (Carol)

PFLAG Western Sydney
Phone 02 9602 9547 (Rudy and Mary)
Information line 02 9294 1002
Email: vdh@iprimus.com.au
www.pflagaustralia.org

PFLAG Bathurst
Phone 02 6332 3685 (Helen) or 02 6331 7267 (Tony)

PFLAG Coffs Harbour
Phone 02 6651 7841 (Vicki)

PFLAG Gunnedah/Tamworth
Phone 02 6769 7552 (Val) or 02 6785 7325 (Fay)

PFLAG Northern Rivers
Phone 02 6687 4726 (Robyn and Richard)

PFLAG Port Macquarie
Phone 02 6585 2791 (Jeanne) or 02 6584 0971 (Gerard)

PFLAG Melbourne
Phone 03 9827 8408
Email: pflagvic@yahoo.com.au
www.geocities.com/WestHollywood/6067

PFLAG Brisbane
Phone 07 3017 1777 (Shelley Argent)

PFLAG Gold Coast
Phone 07 5530 2574 (Pat Fernandes)

PFLAG Rockhampton
07 4928 7275 (Rosemary and Neville)
email: rosiejnevillek@itxtreme.com.au

PFLAG South Australia
Phone 08 8241 0616 (Pam) or 08 8369 0718 (Ralph)
email: pamandon@tpg.com.au or pspflagsa@hotmail.com

PFLAG Tasmania
Phone 03 6234 2372 (Elle)

Acknowledgements

This book is a recognition of the work and efforts, strategies and reflections of dynamic parents, educators, activists and young people coming out in support of GLBT young people. It is with honour and humility that I thank the contributors, interviewees, discussion group and workshop participants, who have kindly allowed years of inspirational activism and rigorous research, healing heartaches and persistent passion, to be shorthanded into this book.

I wish to thank the two inspirational initiators of this project: Lesley McFarlane from the Association of Women Educators (AWE), and Dr Michael Crowhurst from the University of Melbourne. Lesley and Michael were the catalysts to compiling this book. Lesley invited me to edit a 2001 edition of the AWE journal, REDRESS, on 'Sexuality in Education'. Subsequent conversations with Michael about that edition and the need for a larger book led to the development of this book. The passionate activism of friends and colleagues like Lesley and Michael sustains me!

I also wish to thank Adrian Kelly of Transcripts Plus for hours of sensitive and confidential transcribing of interview and group discussion transcripts.

My thanx also to contributors and research participants whose pieces were unable to be included, only because of word limits: Lynn Burnett, Shanton Chang, Greg Curran, Barbara Fox, Maxine Garnsey, Liz Hammond and Leissa from Family Planning NSW, Dominic Herne, Tanya Lavin, Jane Lunt, Nathaniel Maunder, Ian Seal, Jonard Ubalde, Stephanie Walters, and Elke Wooderson. Every one of you is undertaking so much work in your own right and I wish to acknowledge your passion!

I am greatly indebted to dear friends and colleagues who took time out of their own busy lives to assist me in finding research participants and contributors: Dr Lori Beckett, Elena Castrechini, Paul Cordeiro, Jess Heerde, Dominic Herne, Agnes Lichtor, Martin Milani, Rev. Rod Pattenden, Dr George Taleporos.

I am also greatly indebted to the groups of inspirational and passionate parents and young people with whom precious hours were shared. They coordinated and advertised my visits to their group meetings; they made my research discussions more convivial with delicious refreshments; they made sure the audio-taping equipment worked; they undertook the task of chasing up photos. The groups were:

Shlom Eshel and the Pride and Diversity Group

Jemma Mead and Vicki Guglielmo and the YGLAM Youth Group

Parents Supporting PFLAG Group in SA – Ralph Graham and Pam Cooke

PFLAG Sydney – Noel Crehan, Julie and Jeff

PFLAG Victoria – Nan McGregor, Karen Stuart, Geoff Heaviside

PFLAG Western Sydney – Mollie Smith, Keith and Narelle Phipps, Mary and Rudy Vanderhart.

I am moved by the generosity and creativity of Kenton Miller. His cartoons provide the edge, the humour, and that extra insight. It seems like only yesterday I turned up to your Volunteer Training Nights at the South Australian AIDS Council in 1990, Kenton, grieving over the death of a dear friend, and then went on to discover your many talents and beautiful spirit.

Another huge thanx to Sam Trigg, Dianne Jeffrey and Jamie Dunbar for their photography, and for David Lejiz and Patricia Dowma for appearing in Dianne's photos.

It has been a pleasure working with Rex Finch again. His groundedness and his commitment to his authors and their projects are awesome. And of course, I send relieved thanx for Rex's patience as deadline after deadline disappeared, and for his ability to envision possibility amid the vague rambles of an author/academic, and nurture it to its birth as a book.

It has also been a pleasure getting to know Sean Doyle at Finch Publishing and Heather Jamieson, who undertook the patient editing of the manuscript, and my thanx to the saso designers, who brought such vibrancy to these pages.

A huge thanx to the many schools around Australia that have invited me over the years to do 'anti-homophobia work' with staff and students. The discussions and debates have both encouraged and challenged me, and I hope you continue the journeys we undertook together.

My colleagues and students in the School of Health and Social Development, Deakin University, have again sustained me with camaraderie and encouragement, even when I seemed transported elsewhere, in front of my computer screen for hours. They inspire me with their own incredible efforts in making this world more just. My students bring laughter and learning into my life, and have patiently allowed me to trial ideas and questions with them. I wish each one the most exciting and meaningful of journeys in their own lives as educators and health workers.

I am also greatly appreciative of the funding I received as a Small Strategic Research Grant from the Faculty of Health and Behavioural Sciences, Deakin University.

And of course, as always, to my patient and inspirational family and friends who live through the various stages of research, travel and writing that a book such as this involves. Rob and Steph especially, my beacons of light and love, I will never be able to thank you enough for the daily nurturing, laughter and opportunities to relax. You ground me and you make me soar. I only hope I am supporting you at least half as beautifully as you support me.

Contributors

Due to the need for confidentiality, or just feeling that their pieces spoke adequately for them, some contributors chose not to provide further details about themselves. Other contributors wanted you to know a little bit more about themselves and provided contact details, should you wish to get in touch.

James Adcock (page 74) grew up in quiet and conservative suburban Sydney. Since his coming out, his parents have become proud Mardi Gras supporters and celebrate the diversity of their family.

Margaret Ainsworth (page 192) at age 70 has been involved with parents of gay, lesbian and bisexual children for thirteen years, and in the year 2000 walked in the Mardi Gras with other parents and her daughter, Chris. This was a very emotional experience. Margaret writes: 'I have been married for 51 years and have four children, three grandchildren and three great-grandchildren. All my family, including my husband Don, have always been extremely supportive and proud of what I do.'

Joel Baker (page 148) is now nineteen, gay and proud and has been interviewed for Perth's *Out* newspaper. His motto is *carpe diem*, seize the day. Joel writes, 'I would like to thank two people for helping me through my school, giving me the opportunity to communicate my thoughts and opinions, and who supported me when I thought I was all alone: Ms T. Barber and Mr W. Beattie.'

Jen Blyth (page 165) is the editor of *Purple Bus*, a magazine for same-sex attracted young people by same-sex attracted young people (see www.geocities.com/purplebusstop/). She is currently studying Youth Work at RMIT University.

Bryan (page 173)

Jan Coleman (page 78) feels strongly about official Church prejudice against homosexuality and is a committee member of the Rainbow Sash. She is also a keen writer published in several magazines and anthologies.

Pam Cooke (page 16) is a mother of two, grandmother of three. Her interests are playing the piano, singing, and volunteer support work with families with gay children.

Peta Cox (page 168) writes: 'At the time of writing, I was beginning my first relationship and was in Year 11. I'm currently at university doing an Arts/Psychology degree, and working both professionally and as a volunteer to improve the physical and mental wellbeing of GLBT young people.'

Michael Crowhurst, PhD, (page 153) teaches through the Australian Youth Research Centre at Melbourne University. He has written about queer school experiences: http://thesis.lib.unimelb.edu.au/adt-root/public/adt-vu2002.0052/index.html

Jacqui Cussen (page 123) is a secondary school teacher who has recently moved to Indonesia to teach internationally. She has presented information on issues confronting transgender young people at conferences and in publications, and she writes and speaks from research and personal experience.

Pamela Du Valle (pages viii and ix) continues to love and support all gay people, especially gay children. Apart from loving her own son, she is also a mum to two other young gay men who have no family support. You can contact Pamela at tahu007@iprimus.com.au

Mic Emslie (pages 184 and 212) worked as a project worker for Generation Q in the year 2000.

Shlom Eshel (page 146) has qualifications in psychology and social work and has seven years of experience in the youth field. She has worked with same-sex attracted young people for the past four years.

Maria F (page 176) is a passionate mother raising her two children to respect and celebrate diversity. She doesn't want that undermined, and challenges any homophobic community or media attitudes, hoping that this will teach her children to also challenge injustices.

Pamela Garske (page 4) is a wife and mother who found herself and her family in a confusing world for a time, but with lots of reading, learning and finally, understanding love, she is now happy and relaxed. She writes: 'I wish politicians and others in positions of power would be more open minded and prepared to listen.'

John Gascoigne (page 159) is an itinerant poet, playwright and critic. He recently boarded a train for Melbourne, carrying a single suitcase. Contact him at sunshine_bell@hotmail.com.

Geoffrey (page 52) followed a career based in engineering and accounting with a long-term position as Senior Social Worker in a faith-based organisation in Brimbank, a western suburb of Melbourne, where he worked as a counsellor and welfare rights activist before retiring. He is currently doing capacity building in HIV/AIDS work in India and East Africa as an equally worthwhile retirement project.

Gillian (page 24) is a school counsellor with the NSW Department of Education and Training. She's been married 35 years to a lovely Frenchman and has three wonderful adult children. She writes: 'I have learnt and grown so much from my "journey".'

Hayley (page 163) writes: 'After completing secondary school I went to La Trobe University, Victoria, for one year, doing an arts degree. I've now deferred my place to travel the globe for a year or two.

Jess Heerde (page 227) is an Honours student in the School of Health and Social Development at Deakin University, studying in adolescent health. She currently works at a national youth suicide prevention organisation and aims to continue to work in life skills programs for young people and youth suicide prevention.

Shirley and Graham Hughes (page 19) write: 'We are and always will be proud of our son.'

Joanne and *Michael* (page 65)

Johnathan Jones (page 220) is 23 years old and is the youngest ordained minister in the worldwide denomination of Metropolitan Community Churches. Johnathan's passion is working with and for young people.

Lauren (pages 8 and 224)

Agnes Lichtor (pages 170, 186 and 225) has a strong passion for social justice and equal opportunity for all. She is involved in a number of initiatives working with young people and the wider community, and is currently studying a Masters of Public Health in the Faculty of Health and Behavioural Sciences at Deakin University, Melbourne. She can be contacted on: aal@deakin.edu.au.

Lian Low (page 120) is completing a Diploma of Arts (Professional Writing and Editing) at RMIT TAFE and a Certificate IV in Multimedia at Swinburne TAFE. Hopefully she will find a job that she is passionate about one day, otherwise she will never stop being a student.

Clare Lyons (page 114) has taught religious education in a variety of Catholic schools and continues to study in the areas of theology and student welfare. She has completed her Masters of Education thesis, 'A New Way of Thinking: Gay Students in Catholic Schools'. Clare can be contacted by email: clyons12@bigpond.com.

Madelaine and *Luciano* (page 108) have both completed arts degrees at Monash University. After working in schools for six years, they undertook postgraduate diplomas in secondary education, and at the time of publication, they were both teaching in Victorian secondary schools.

Nan McGregor (page 102) has four adult children, one of whom is gay. She has been President of PFLAG Victoria since its incorporation and travels around as a guest speaker on its behalf, while also preparing the PFLAG newsletter and helping staff the help line. In 1996, she was awarded a Rainbow Award in the Category of Care and Support, which also acknowledged the work PFLAG undertakes. She is also a member of the Rainbow Sash Movement, has marched in all Pride Marches, in five Mardi Gras Parades, four of them with her son and his partner, and three with her straight daughter, Anne.

Caz McLean (page 178) is currently working at Kingston City Council as a Senior Community Services Planner and is in the final year of a Master of Social Science – Policy and Human Services, at Royal Melbourne Institute of Technology.

Kirsten McLean, PhD, (page 126) is a lecturer in Sociology at Monash University, Melbourne. Her research interests include bisexuality, sexuality theory and youth studies. She can be contacted by email: Kirsten.Mclean@arts.monash.edu.au.

Wayne Martino, PhD, (page 200) is a senior lecturer in the School of Education, Murdoch University, Perth, Western Australia. His latest books are *Being Normal is the Only Way To Be: Student Perspectives on Gender and Schooling* co-authored with Maria Pallotta-Chiarolli, and *Gendered Outcasts: Interrogating Sexual Oppression and Gender Hierarchies in Queer Men's Lives* co-authored with Christopher Kendall.

Jemma Mead and *Vicky Guglielmo* (page 182) coordinate YGLAM Performing Arts Project, a Moreland Community Health Service program for 14- to 25-year-old same-sex attracted youth.

Kenton Miller (pages 3 and ff.) identifies as a gay man who happens to be a cartoonist. He has worked at the AIDS Council of South Australia (ACSA), The Second Story Youth Health Service (SA), the Victorian AIDS Council/Gay Men's Health Centre (VAC/GMHC), The Cancer Council of Victoria (TCCV) and at VicHealth in Peer Education and Health Promotion. Along the way, he has produced many health promotion resources such as the national 'BLOCKOUT/Challenging Homophobia' training kit with his friend Mahamati. He has also been the media spokesperson for Lesbian and Gay Community Action (LGCA) and the male co-convenor for the Victorian Gay and Lesbian Rights Lobby (VGLRL). While he has been the cartoonist for many gay publications as well as illustrating several manuals and books (e.g. *Understanding Adolescents, Peace or Pieces: A Non-Violent Parenting Manual*), he currently does cartoons for his own sanity and commercial gain. Some of the cartoons in this book appeared in this or similar form in either *Outrage* magazine (published by Bluestone Media) or in *Not Round Here: Affirming Diversity, Challenging Homophobia – Rural Service Providers' Training Manual* by Kenton Penley Miller and Mahamati (published by HREOC, 2000). He can be contacted at kenton_miller@hotmail.com.

Karla Mokros (page 209) believes every parent should love their gay children as unconditionally as she and her husband love their son.

Narelle (page 72) was a very unhappy mother when she discovered her son is gay. She writes: 'Becoming involved with PFLAG and gaining understanding has completely changed my attitude and life.' Email: help@pflagaustralia.org.

Vittorio Perri (page 206) writes: 'I hope my small contribution can give strength and confidence to other young men who are dealing with the same issues.'

Pride and Diversity Youth Group (page 146)

Jackie Ruddock (page 132) is currently working directly with GLBT young people as a group worker. She remains committed to the importance of inclusivity in education systems and wider communities.

Sandra and *Leanne* (page 104)

Sebastian (page 150)

Adele Shaheed (pages 10 and 92) writes: 'Since these letters were written, we've all become even closer. As a single parent with all my extended family in the USA, I feel very fortunate to have such wonderful children. We all lead very busy, sociable and meaningful lives.'

Karen Stuart (page 101) writes: 'I'm an ordinary mum with a love for all my children. I have been a member of PFLAG for eleven years, supporting other parents going through difficulties accepting their son/daughter's homosexuality.'

Susan (pages 70 and 98) writes: 'I'm a very proud mum of two sons who happen to be gay. My husband and our sons are one happy and blessed family. How lucky are we?'

T (pages 40 and 204) is a medical interpreter who has a strong interest in the health of ethnic minorities. She has lived in Australia for eight years.

Tony (page 202)

Sam Trigg is a South Australian artist/photographer who specialises in handmade greeting cards and papercrafts, sold under the name of Ramillies Papercrafts. He photographs anything that moves and a lot that doesn't! He can be contacted by email: sjntrigg@hotmail.com.

Rudy and *Mary Vanderhart* (page 33)

Abe Whyte's mum, *Rose*, (page 84) writes: 'Abe is a fine young man, continuing with his studies and commitment to social justice. Abe agrees with this.'

Luke Williams (page 198)

Daniel Witthaus (page 137) currently lives and works in Melbourne. In between travel adventures, he runs workshops on sexual diversity and homophobia for young people, teachers and workers. Daniel can be contacted at daniel@prideandprejudice.com.au.

Yellowkitties (pages 40 and 204)

YGLAM Youth Group (pages 39, 158, 182 and 226)

Hilarie Zwaller, PhD, (page 135) is a science teacher in a Victorian state school who still gets asked awkward questions by students. She is heartened by the recent progress made by schools in the support and recognition of diversity. Hilarie writes: 'It is only through care and respect for others that one realises their humanity.'

Other Finch titles of interest

Girls' Talk

Young women speak their hearts and minds
Edited by Maria Pallotta-Chiarolli
Girls want a book that gets real about the issues in their lives. Here 150 young women tell it like it is. A riveting read – credible, direct and heartwarming.
ISBN 1876451 025

Adolescence

A guide for parents
Michael Carr-Gregg and Erin Shale
In this informative and wide-ranging book, the authors help parents understand what is happening for young people aged 10–20 and how to deal with it. They discuss the big questions in a young person's life and provide parents and teachers with useful approaches for handling problems.
ISBN 1876451 351

Raising Girls

Why girls are different – and how to help them grow up happy and strong
Gisela Preuschoff injects her own experiences as mother of four into this book, and illustrates her points with stories and examples from the experiences of many families. Her advice ranges from birth to late adolescence – and across physical and sexual development, schools and learning, gender stereotyping, parent–child relationships and the daughter's emotional life.
ISBN 1876451 599

Teen Stages

How to guide their journey to adulthood
Ken & Elizabeth Mellor
Teenagers need lots of attention in the early to middle years and actually want to be controlled. One of the Mellors' key concepts is that teenagers grow through six very developmental stages, each requiring specific responses that rarely work for the others. To help parents and teachers, the Mellors offer numerous practical, tested suggestions about what to do. They also give many simple hints on how to deal with 'trouble' and, better still, how to head it off before it starts.
ISBN 1876451 386

Raising Boys

Why boys are different – and how to help them become
happy and well-balanced men (2nd edition)
In his international bestseller, Steve Biddulph examines the crucial ways that boys differ from girls. He looks at boys' development from birth to manhood and discusses the warm, strong parenting and guidance boys need.
ISBN 1 876451 505
Raising Boys Audio A double-cassette set read by Steve Biddulph.
ISBN 1 876451 254

Bullybusting

How to help children deal with teasing and bullying
Evelyn Field reveals the 'six secrets of bullybusting', which contain important life skills for any young person. Activities introduce young readers to new skills in communicating feelings, responding to stressful situations and building a support network. An empowering book for parents and their children (5-16 years).
ISBN 1876451 041

Confident Parenting

*How to set limits, be considerate
and stay in charge*
Dr William Doherty
'We may be the most child-sensitive generations of parents the world has ever known –
and the most confused and insecure,' says the
author. This book shows you how to parent
effectively and how to ensure that your family is not overwhelmed by external pressures
such as advertising, TV, and peer culture.
ISBN 1876451 467

Stepfamily Life

*Why it is different – and how to
make it work*
In this book, Margaret Newman, an experienced couple and family counsellor and a
member of a stepfamily herself, describes
challenges that members of a stepfamily usually encounter. In her experience, stepfamily
life is different, and therefore different solutions are needed to get it 'on track' – and,
more importantly, to help it survive. Margaret
considers a wide range of stepfamily scenarios, and gives practical suggestions as to
what to do in each case to overcome any
difficulties.
ISBN 1876451 521

On Their Own

Boys growing up underfathered
Rex McCann
For a young man, growing up without an
involved father in his life can leave a powerful
sense of loss. On Their Own considers the
needs of young men as they mature, the pas-
sage from boyhood to manhood, and the roles
of fathers and mothers.
ISBN 1876451 084

Emotional Fitness

Facing yourself, facing the world
Cynthia Morton tells her own abusive story
and outlines her innovative program of 30
'emotional workouts', which forms the back-
bone of this book. These workouts are tai-
lored for different stages along the path to
emotional recovery and have been successfully used in sessions with individuals and
groups. They help individuals learn how
to overcome difficult issues in their lives,
care for themselves and ultimately reach
self-acceptance.
ISBN 1876451 580

Bouncing Back

*How to overcome setbacks, become resilient
and create a happier life*
In this practical book, Brian Babington, a
counsellor specialising in grief and loss, outlines some approaches to cope with the initial
trauma of loss and failure – and to find ways
to recover. His approaches will help people
who have experienced severe loss – such as
a death in the family – or other traumatic
events, such as the breakdown of a relationship or the loss of a job.
ISBN 1876451 564

Journeys in Healing

*How others have triumphed over disease
and disability*
Dr Shaun Matthews takes us into the lives of
eight people who have suffered life-altering
illness or disability. Their stories present
empowering messages for all sufferers of disease and disability, and demonstrate the
interconnectedness between physical, mental,
emotional and spiritual health.
ISBN 1876451 424

Sex-life Solutions

How to solve everyday sexual problems
Respected sex therapist Dr Janet Hall offers
clear and practical step-by-step directions for
solving all types of sexual difficulties. The
book includes sections for men, women,
and couples, as well as one on anxieties
based on mixed messages and misunder-
standings about sex.
ISBN 1876451 408

Take Control of Your Life

*The five-step plan to health and happiness
(2nd edition)*
Dr Gail Ratcliffe
This book is a blueprint for recognising what
is wrong with your life, minimising your
stress and maximising the opportunities to
reach your goals. The author, a clinical psychologist, has developed her five-step method
of life-planning and stress management with
clients for over 13 years.
ISBN 1 876451 513

Manhood

*An action plan for changing men's lives (3rd
edition)*
Steve Biddulph tackles the key areas of a
man's life – parenting, love and sexuality,
finding meaning in work, and making real
friends. He presents new pathways to healing
the past and forming true partnerships with
women, as well as honouring our own inner
needs.
ISBN 1876451 203

Dealing with Anger

Self-help solutions for men
Frank Donovan
Focussing on emotional healing and practical
change, this book includes case studies from
clients of the author's (a psychotherapist) and
a program of exercises for the reader.
ISBN 1876451 05X

The Body Snatchers

How the media shapes women
Cyndi Tebbel
From childhood, women are told they can
never be too thin or too young. The author
exposes the rampant conditioning of women
and girls by those pushing starvation
imagery, and encourages us to challenge
society's preoccupation with an ideal body
that is unnatural and (for most) unattainable.
ISBN 1876451 076

Blood Ties

The stories of five positive women
Edited by Salli Trathen
This collection of the stories of five Australian
HIV-positive women reveals how each
woman approached her predicament, and
the inner qualities she drew on to persevere.
The authors' honest and courageous writing
allows us to live with them through their
struggles. What emerges is a triumph of the
human spirit over adversity.
ISBN 1 876451 297

The Partner Test

How well are the two of you suited?
In this entertaining and informative book,
designed for the under-40s, Jo Lamble & Sue
Morris aim to give couples insights into their
relationship. Twenty tests cover important
issues associated with attraction, compatibili-
ty, commitment, life together, intimacy and
sex, communication and expectations.
ISBN 1876451 602

Online and Personal

The reality of Internet relationships
With the boom in Internet dating services
and chat rooms, the authors, Jo Lamble and
Sue Morris, offer guidelines for Net users to
protect themselves, their relationships and
their children from the hazards that exist
online.
ISBN 1876451 173

Surviving Year 12

A sanity kit for students and their parents
Michael Carr-Gregg
In this book for students facing the pressures of Year 12, the author uses humour and worldly wisdom to explore the key issues: keeping it all in perspective; studying smarter; overcoming stress; getting enough sleep; setting goals; the roles of relaxation, exercise and diet; and coping with the exams themselves. He advises parents that nagging is itself a major stressor.
ISBN 1876451 53X

Boys in Schools

Addressing the real issues – behaviour, values and relationships
Edited by Rollo Browne and Richard Fletcher
Positive accounts of how classroom teachers have implemented innovative approaches to help boys' learning and their understanding of relationships.
ISBN 0646239 589

Life Smart

Choices for young people about friendship, family and future
Vicki Bennett
This highly acclaimed book for teenagers provides a valuable perspective and sound advice on how to deal with the most pressing issues of those vital years – the ups and downs of friendship and love, learning to accept ourselves and others, creating a direction in our lives, and relating to our families.
ISBN 1876451 130

Twelve Principles

Living with integrity in the twenty-first century
For a world seeking moral leadership, Tasmanian environmentalist Martin Hawes proposes ways by which we can live responsibly, reappraise our values, and develop a global consciousness. Includes profiles of inspiring people from around the world.
ISBN 1876451 483

For further information on these and all of our titles, visit our website:
www.finch.com.au

Index